EUGENE O'NEILL

Born in New York City in 1888, son of a well-known actor, Eugene O'Neill spent a year at Princeton University (1906) before signing on as a seaman and travelling widely. Following a period in a sanatorium recovering from TB, he wrote his first play, *A Wife for a Life*. In 1916 he joined the Provincetown Players, who produced the first of his plays to be staged, *Bound East for Cardiff*, as well as other early work. His Broadway debut came in 1920 with *Beyond the Horizon*, which also won him a Pulitzer Prize.

The next fourteen years saw the premieres of some twenty new plays, including *The Emperor Jones* (1920), *Anna Christie* (1921), which won a second Pulitzer Prize, *The Hairy Ape* (1922), *All God's Chillun Got Wings* (1924), *Desire Under the Elms* (1924), *The Great God Brown* (1926), *Strange Interlude* (1928), which won another Pulitzer, *Mourning Becomes Electra* (1931), a trilogy reworking the *Oresteia*, *Ah! Wilderness* (1933) and *Days Without End* (1933), after which thirteen years elapsed with no new play reaching the stage, though he continued writing. Two more plays were produced during his lifetime: *The Iceman Cometh* in 1946, though written in 1939, and *A Moon for the Misbegotten* in 1947, though it only reached Broadway ten years later, after his death in 1953.

Plays staged posthumously include *Long Day's Journey into Night* (1956), which won a fourth Pulitzer, *A Touch of the Poet* (1958) and *More Stately Mansions* (1962). He was three times married, his third wife, Carlotta Monterey, surviving him. In 1936 he became the first American dramatist to win the Nobel Prize for Literature.

D0715210

In the same series

Long Day's Journey into Night
Anna Christie & The Emperor Jones
Strange Interlude
Mourning Becomes Electra

In preparation

The Hairy Ape & All God's Chillun Got Wings
Desire Under the Elms & The Great God Brown
Ah! Wilderness
A Touch of the Poet
The Iceman Cometh

EUGENE O'NEILL
A MOON FOR THE MISBEGOTTEN

Introduction by
Christine Dymkowski

NT

ROYAL NATIONAL THEATRE
London

N H B

NICK HERN BOOKS

A Moon for the Misbegotten first published in this edition in 1992 jointly by the Royal National Theatre, London, and Nick Hern Books, a Random Century Company, 20 Vauxhall Bridge Road, London SW1V 2SA

First published in Great Britain by Jonathan Cape in 1953
Copyright © 1945 by Eugene O'Neill

Introduction, Biographical Sketch of Eugene O'Neill and List of Produced Plays Copyright © 1992 by Christine Dymkowski

Cover photograph of Eugene O'Neill by courtesy of the Raymond Mander & Joe Mitcheson Theatre Collection

Set in Baskerville by 🄰 Tek Art Ltd,
Addiscombe, Croydon, Surrey
Printed by Cox & Wyman Ltd, Reading, Berkshire

British Library Cataloguing in Publication Data: a catalogue record for this book is available from the British Library

ISBN 1 85459 139 8

Biographical Sketch of Eugene O'Neill (1888–1953)

'Some day James O'Neill will best be known as the father of Eugene O'Neill': so Eugene himself frequently boasted throughout 1912. The claim struck those who heard it not with a sense of the young man's prescience but of his presumption. Nothing in his life so far had given any indication that in less than a decade he would be a playwright to reckon with, shaking up the American theatre and shaping a new American drama. Instead, he seemed more likely to become one of the pipe-dreamers who eternally inhabit Harry Hope's no-chance saloon in his own *The Iceman Cometh*.

Born on 16 October 1888, to the respected and accomplished actor James O'Neill and his wife Ella Quinlan O'Neill, Eugene was to find his family an overwhelming force in his life and to make it the almost constant subject of his plays. He was the O'Neills' third son: the eldest, Jamie, had been born ten years before; a second son, Edmund, had followed five years later. Life was not easy for the O'Neills and their two young children; James was already touring the country in *Monte Cristo*, the vehicle that would spell both his financial success and his artistic defeat (he succumbed to popular demand and played the role 4000 times between 1883 and 1912). Ella, convent-educated and proper, loved her husband but felt she had married beneath her; she never took to James's theatrical life or to his theatrical friends. However, the couple could not bear to be parted, and Ella, with great reluctance, frequently left the children in the care of her mother to join her husband on the road. Early in 1885, on one of these occasions, Jamie contracted measles and disobeyed instructions to stay away from his brother; Edmund became ill and died.

Such family history might in another case seem irrelevant, but it is crucial for an understanding of Eugene O'Neill and of his work. Ella did not want any more children after Edmund's death, but James, convinced that it would help solace her, persuaded her to have another. The result was a family tragedy that blighted all four lives, and not least the new baby, Eugene. In an attempt to counteract the pain of an exceedingly difficult birth, Ella was unwittingly precipitated into the morphine addiction from which she would suffer for the next twenty-six years. James, Jamie, and Eugene were greatly affected by Ella's distraction and withdrawal from reality, but Jamie and Eugene endured a private hell of guilt: Jamie for inadvertently killing the brother whose loss had had such drastic consequences, and Eugene for having been born at all.

Fifteen when he learned of his mother's addiction, Eugene no longer had to fear the mental illness he had up till then suspected he would inherit; the truth, however, was worse. Although summers were spent at the family's home in New London, Connecticut, their haphazard existence in a succession of hotels while James was on tour had already given Eugene a sense of rootlessness that plagued him all his life. Now, guilty that his birth had effected such misery, he developed a deep sense of unbelonging that at times manifested itself as a death-wish. He rejected his parents' Catholicism and, under Jamie's influence, began to drink and to visit brothels. Both Jamie and Eugene, displacing their anger, blamed their father for their mother's condition, accusing him of hiring a 'quack' to attend Ella at Eugene's birth. In fact, even reputable doctors at that time prescribed morphine, and in doses so low that addiction was by no means inevitable.

Eugene entered Princeton in 1906, but only stayed a year, having spent most of his time drinking, cutting classes, and following his own reading interests. It was at this time that he discovered Nietzsche's *Thus Spake Zarathustra*, which together with the works of Strindberg, became his personal bible. After leaving Princeton, he worked for a short time in a New York office job arranged by his father. In the city's Greenwich Village, Hell's Kitchen, and Tenderloin districts, he began to frequent the dives he would immortalise in many of his plays and also began to write poetry. O'Neill remained a heavy drinker for years, though he never drank while writing; in 1926 he gave up alcohol completely, lapsing only a few times thereafter.

Wishing to escape from a romantic entanglement with Kathleen Jenkins, O'Neill let his father arrange for him to join a mining expedition in Honduras in October 1909. Nevertheless, because Kathleen was pregnant, he agreed to marry her shortly before his departure. Having contracted malaria after a few months in Central America, Eugene returned to the US and, without visiting his wife and new-born son (Eugene O'Neill, Jr.), joined his father's company on tour, checking tickets. Shortly afterwards, in June 1910, O'Neill boarded the *Charles Racine*, a Norwegian windjammer, as a working passenger on its two-month voyage to

Buenos Aires. O'Neill loved the sea – he was throughout his life a keen and able swimmer – and now had the chance to experience a sailing life first-hand; it was an experience he would exploit in many of his early plays.

O'Neill remained in Argentina for several months, occasionally working but mainly living as a down-and-out; he sailed back to New York in March 1911 on the S.S. *Ikala*, this time as a member of the crew. He stayed in New York long enough to arrange for a divorce, living in an alcoholic haze at a downtown bar and flophouse called Jimmy-the-Priest's. In July, he signed onto the S.S. *New York* as an ordinary seaman for its voyage to Southampton; he returned in August on the S.S. *Philadelphia* as an able-bodied seaman, a qualification of which he was to remain proud for the rest of his life. Resuming his destitute way of life at Jimmy-the-Priest's – though he regularly attended the performances of Dublin's Abbey Players, who were visiting New York – O'Neill sank progressively into a depression that in January 1912 culminated in a suicide attempt. When he had sufficiently recovered, he rejoined his father's company for a few months, this time taking on small acting roles.

1912 seemed to mark a watershed in O'Neill's life, as evidenced both by his boasting of future fame and by his setting of many of his most autobiographical plays in that year. Moving to New London, Connecticut, in the summer, he worked as a reporter for the *Telegraph*, continued to write poetry, and developed a mild case of tuberculosis. By the end of the year, he was at the Gaylord Farm Sanatorium, where he was to remain for six months. During that time he decided to become a playwright.

Returning to New London in summer 1913 and boarding with the Rippins, a local family, he began to write one-act plays based on his own experiences. O'Neill's father subsidised their publication as *Thirst and Other One Act Plays* in August 1914, and the following September O'Neill enrolled in Professor George Pierce Baker's famous play-writing course at Harvard. Although he did not particularly distinguish himself in the class, his disdain for easy formulaic success made clear his ambition to be an original dramatist.

After his year at Harvard, O'Neill returned to New York and became somewhat involved in the political and intellectual life of Greenwich Village, frequenting the Golden Swan saloon, familiarly known as the 'Hell Hole'. He submitted some plays to the adventurous Washington Square Players, who had recently formed in reaction to the glib, commercial offerings of Broadway; however, the Players were not so adventurous as to stage any of O'Neill's works.

His first real theatrical opportunity came in June 1916 when he accompanied his friend Terry Carlin to Provincetown, at the tip of Massachusetts's Cape Cod. Then, as now, Provincetown boasted a flourishing artists' colony each summer. The previous year, the writer Susan Glaspell, her husband Jig Cook, and other vacationing Greenwich Village friends had staged an impromptu production, marking the birth of what would become the Provincetown Players. When O'Neill arrived in Provincetown, the group were desperately short of plays for their new season. O'Neill offered them *Bound East for Cardiff*, which premiered on 28 July 1916, the first-ever performance of an O'Neill play. His work with the Players also led to his involvement in Greenwich Village's radical circle, which included John Reed, Louise Bryant, Mabel Dodge, and Floyd Dell, among others.

The Provincetown Players' success was such that in September 1916 they moved operations to Greenwich Village, acquiring a base on Macdougal Street, which at O'Neill's suggestion was named the Playwrights' Theatre. During the group's eight subscription seasons between 1916 and 1922, O'Neill had ample opportunity to experiment without regard to commercial considerations. For example, *The Emperor Jones*, staged by the Provincetown Players in November 1920, not only had an African-American for its protagonist but was also considerably shorter than standard length. Despite its unconventionality, the play marked the group's first popular success: following its scheduled performances at the Playwrights' Theatre, it moved uptown to Broadway for an unlimited run. When the original Provincetown Players disbanded, O'Neill, together with the designer Robert Edmond Jones and the critic-producer Kenneth Macgowan, founded the Experimental Theatre, Inc., in 1923. The triumvirate ran the Playwrights' Theatre, now renamed the Provincetown Playhouse, from 1923–25 and the Greenwich Village Theatre from 1924–26.

The Provincetown Players' success with *The Emperor Jones* was not O'Neill's first theatrical triumph. *Beyond the Horizon*, which opened at the Morosco Theatre on Broadway in February 1920, was greeted by extremely favourable reviews, transferred for an extended run, and brought O'Neill his first Pulitzer Prize (the second drama award in the prize's four-year history). This success was quickly followed by another: *Anna Christie* opened in November 1921 and brought him a second Pulitzer. He was to win the award twice more, for *Strange Interlude* in 1928 and posthumously in 1956 for *Long Day's Journey into Night*, a record that has not been matched.

By the time of his early success, O'Neill's personal life had undergone considerable change: married for a second time, to the writer Agnes Boulton, he had become a father again with the birth of Shane Rudraighe O'Neill on 30 October 1919 (his last child, Oona, who later married Charlie Chaplin, was born on 14 May 1925). His father had died in August 1920, having lived long enough to see his younger son succeed; in the year prior to his death, Eugene had finally recognised his father's long-standing forbearance and support and had become friendly with him. Ironically, O'Neill's own neediness so dominated his life that he could never be a father to his own children, who all suffered the neglect for which O'Neill had bitterly and unfairly resented his own father. Eugene Jr. committed suicide at the age of forty, and Shane was for many years a heroin addict.

Within three years of his father's death, O'Neill was the sole survivor of his original family: his mother died of a brain tumour in February 1922, and Jamie had drunk himself to death by November 1923. Their deaths freed O'Neill to explore the dark side of his family life, which he proceeded to do in plays as diverse (and variously successful) as *All God's Chillun Got Wings*, *Dynamo*, *Long Day's Journey into Night*, and *A Moon for the Misbegotten*. Further change was in store: in 1927 O'Neill left Agnes Boulton for Carlotta Monterey, who became his third wife in July 1929. Misogynist, desirous of a mother, unable to separate love from hate, O'Neill had difficult relationships with women. He found his own guilt at his desertion of Agnes too difficult to deal with, and, as he later did with his children, manufactured grievances against her. His third marriage fulfilled his desire that his wife should be completely dedicated to his own interests, but it was a stormy one with cruelty on both sides.

O'Neill was quintessentially an autobiographical playwright: many of his protagonists are recognisable O'Neill figures, sharing the playwright's own lean build and dark deep-set eyes. All of his experiences found their way onto the stage, from the sea-going life depicted in early one-act plays like *Bound East for Cardiff* to his ambivalence about parenthood in *The First Man* to his Strindbergian view of marital relations in *Welded*. This need to depict, explain, and justify himself had considerable ramifications for his role as a playwright: he could not really regard theatre as the collaborative activity it so patently is. Time and again. O'Neill lamented the process of staging his plays, complaining that the ideal play he had seen in his head never existed in production. Whereas playwrights generally welcome the new life that actors and directors bring to their work, O'Neill saw it as a betrayal. So strongly did he feel this that he virtually never went to any productions of his plays, only attending rehearsals in order to advise and to cut when necessary.

In addition, his personal investment in what he wrote often blinded him to its deficiencies: he could be convinced that inferior works like *Welded*, *Dynamo*, and *Days Without End* were undervalued and misjudged. For example, while *Dynamo* ostensibly focused on the relationship between humankind, machines, and religion, it was really O'Neill's working out of his ambivalent relationship to his mother: small wonder that it made more sense to O'Neill than to the critics. However, at his best, O'Neill was able to transmute his personal experiences into the most powerful of dramas, as he does in works like *Long Day's Journey into Night* and *The Iceman Cometh*.

Although he wrote essentially to please himself and to exorcise his private demons (as early as 1924 he claimed that 'Writing is my vacation from living'), O'Neill was genuinely interested in stretching American drama beyond the narrow confines it had so far inhabited. His experiments were many: trying to make the audience share a character's hallucination in *Where the Cross is Made*, extending the audience's endurance by writing four- and five-hour long plays, using set location schematically in *Beyond the Horizon*, incorporating expressionistic elements in *The Hairy Ape*, masking the characters in *The Great God Brown*, modernising the use of the aside in *Strange Interlude*, developing a modern equivalent for the Greek sense of tragedy in *Desire Under the Elms* and *Mourning Becomes Electra*, creating an ambitious play-cycle detailing a critical history of America through the story of one family in *A Tale of Possessors Self-Dispossessed* (of which only *A Touch of the Poet* was completed to his satisfaction).

Although his achievements won him the Nobel Prize for literature in 1936, in the last years of his life O'Neill was something of a has-been. He had suffered for years from a hand tremor, caused by a rare degenerative disease of the cerebellum that attacks the motor system, which made writing increasingly difficult; by 1943, it had become impossible. Since O'Neill had never been able to compose at a typewriter or by dictation, his writing career, apart from some revisions, was effectively over. Furthermore, he was extremely depressed by the Second World War: it made his writing seem of little consequence and the staging of his work even less important and appropriate. Consequently, he refused to authorise productions of new plays; none appeared between *Days Without End* in 1933 and *The Iceman*

Cometh in 1946. When the latter was finally staged, the inadequate production did little to restore interest in O'Neill's work.

Throughout his life, O'Neill had roamed far in search of a home and a sense of belonging: New York, Connecticut, Provincetown, Bermuda, France, Georgia, California. Sometime before his death on 27 November 1953, O'Neill struggled up from his bed to complain 'I knew it, I knew it! Born in a goddam hotel room and dying in a hotel room!' Only with the posthumous revival of *The Iceman Cometh* and the first production of *Long Day's Journey into Night* in 1956 did his reputation, like his life, come full circle.

Christine Dymkowski
Lecturer in Drama and Theatre Studies
Royal Holloway and Bedford New College
University of London

Introduction to the Play

A Moon for the Misbegotten was the last play O'Neill ever
completed. As the playwright's work diary for 1941 makes clear,
its origin lay in Edmund's anecdote about Shaughnessy the pig-
farmer in Act I of *A Long Day's Journey into Night*. Its focus,
however, was to be O'Neill's brother, again called James Tyrone
Jr. as he was in the earlier play: 'here Jamie principal character &
story of play otherwise entirely imaginary, except for J.'s
revelation of self' (28 October, quoted in Floyd, *Eugene O'Neill at
Work*, p. 371). As usual, O'Neill's 'entirely' is rather over-
emphatic, since the play is peopled not only by his brother (who
had behaved just as the character in the play did when
accompanying his mother's body on the train) but by his friends
and acquaintances as well. Phil Hogan is an incarnation of James
O'Neill Sr.'s tenant-farmer, 'Dirty' Dolan, while T. Stedman
Harder is an amalgam of Edward C. Hammond and of Standard
Oil heir Edward S. Harkness, both of whom had large estates
near O'Neill's New London, Connecticut, home; the episode of
the pigs-in-the-ice-pond was an actual occurrence. Josie Hogan
owes much of her character and some of her physique to
Christine Ell, O'Neill's Greenwich Village friend, who had had an
affair with Jamie some years before his death. In her selfless
assumption of maternal tenderness towards the man she loves,
Josie fulfils some of O'Neill's deepest wishes; however, as several
reviewers and critics have pointed out, she is also in some ways a
wishful self-portrait of the playwright, offering Jamie the
forgiving benediction that O'Neill had been unable to extend to
his brother in life.

   Although O'Neill was already seriously incapacitated by the
illness that would soon make writing an impossibility, work on *A
Moon* initially progressed well. He had written the scenario by 3
November, and four days later began Act I, completing it on 26
November. However, the escalation of World War II with the
Japanese attack on Pearl Harbor on 7 December 1941 depressed
him and made him feel his writing was unimportant; he finished
the first draft on 20 January 1942 but was dissatisfied with it. As
he wrote to the critic Dudley Nichols later that year, 'After [Pearl
Harbor], I couldn't concentrate. Managed to finish the first draft

but the heart was out of it. Haven't looked at it since. There is a fine unusual tragic comedy in *A Moon for the Misbegotten* but it will have to wait until I can rewrite the lifeless post-Pearl Harbor part of it' (16 December 1942, quoted in Bogard & Bryer's *Selected Letters*, p. 538).

O'Neill turned his attention to other projects, among them the one-act *Hughie* and the cycle play *A Touch of the Poet*, before resuming work on *A Moon* early in January 1943. By mid-May, he had finished the second draft, but he continued to revise and polish it throughout the rest of the year and into the following one. One of the significant later changes, made in 1943, is the setting of the play in early September 1923, just two months before Jamie O'Neill's death on 8 November; as Virginia Floyd points out, the decision seems to signal O'Neill's intention 'to make this autobiographical play an epitaph for his brother' (*Eugene O'Neill at Work*, p. 377).

O'Neill offered the play, together with *The Iceman Cometh* and *A Touch of the Poet*, to the Theater Guild, which received them enthusiastically. *The Iceman* was produced first, opening in New York in October 1946, while the Guild launched a search for an actor to play Josie. Apart from the difficulties of finding someone who fitted O'Neill's description of the nearly six-foot-tall, thirteen-stone woman, the Guild were further hampered by O'Neill's insistence that the play's director and actors should be of Irish descent. Mary Welch eventually won the part and O'Neill's approval, despite her lack of size, because she was able to 'project . . . [Josie's] inner state'. Nevertheless, O'Neill had an unusual clause inserted into her contract: 'The artist agrees to gain the necessary weight required for the role' (see Welch's account, reprinted in Cargill, pp. 88–89).

Rehearsals for the new play did not go well; the Guild's directorate (Theresa Helburn, Lawrence Langner, and Armina Marshall) were worried about Welch's lack of experience, while O'Neill complained that James Dunn was not making Jim Tyrone enough of a gentleman. Langner defended Dunn, arguing that he was playing the role as O'Neill had written it. The play's director, Arthur Shields of the Abbey Theatre, Dublin, was only hired after the play had been cast and found himself working with actors he would not himself have chosen. In addition, he believed an author's manuscript was sacrosanct and refused to suggest any cuts, even though O'Neill himself asked whether he should make any.

Given these problems, it was decided that *A Moon* should open out-of-town before appearing on Broadway; it premiered at the Hartman Theater in Columbus, Ohio, on 20 February 1947, before going on to Cleveland, Detroit, Pittsburgh, and St Louis, where it closed on 29 March after roughly 30 performances. Public response to the play was not positive: a group of Irish theatre-goers, feeling insulted by the play's depiction of their compatriots, left half-way through the opening-night performance, while the righteous citizens of Pittsburgh and Detroit objected to what they saw as the play's vulgarity; the police censor of the latter city particularly resented the use of the words 'mother' and 'prostitute' in the same sentence.

Critical reaction, albeit mixed, was more generous: the critic for *Time* magazine, although judging the play rough in spots and in need of pruning, found it 'a far more impressive play than *The Iceman Cometh*' (3 March 1947, p. 47). This critic also quotes the reviews in Ohio newspapers, which, apart from one dismissal of the play as 'unimportant', hailed it as a 'towering achievement', 'harsh [and] powerful' with some of O'Neill's 'best and most touching writing', and 'beautiful in its very ugliness' (Columbus *Citizen*, Columbus *Dispatch*, Cleveland *Plain Dealer*, and *Ohio State Journal* respectively). The *New York Times* greeted with relief O'Neill's writing of a play 'conventional in form for a change and clear and forceful in the reading' (21 February 1947 p. 16).

Given the need for more work on the play and the Guild's dissatisfaction with the leading actors, plans for a Broadway opening were abandoned. The Theater Guild intended to present *A Moon* in a new production directed by Elia Kazan once O'Neill had done the necessary rewriting, but the playwright's failing health and own growing dislike of the play meant that such revision was never accomplished. In 1952, O'Neill published the play as originally written. *A Moon for the Misbegotten* subsequently enjoyed a successful Festival Week production at the Royal Dramatic Theatre, Stockholm, in June 1953; in the following year, it was produced at the Berlin Festival.

It was several years before the play was again seen in the United States; a production by a new repertory group called The Ensemble planned for the 1954/55 season never materialised. *A Moon* finally received its New York premiere, some years after O'Neill's death, on 2 May 1957 at the Bijou Theater; directed by Carmen Capalbo, it starred Wendy Hiller as Josie, Franchot Tone as Jim, and Cyril Cusack as Hogan. By this time, O'Neill was very much back in theatrical fashion: the Circle in the Square production of *The Iceman Cometh* was in its second year, and *Long*

Day's Journey had been playing for several months. There was even a musical version of *Anna Christie*, called *New Girl in Town*, about to open in a few days' time.

A Moon suffered by comparison with the two O'Neill masterpieces already on offer: the *Wall Street Journal*'s Richard P. Cooke dubbed *A Moon* 'minor O'Neill, showing the touches of greatness' (6 May 1957, p. 12), while the *New York Times*'s Brooks Atkinson judged it a 'prolix, uneventful play' with low vitality, rambling dialogue, minor incidents, and maudlin drinking (3 May 1957, p. 21). However, the second half of the play was enthusiastically received by many commentators: Walter Kerr, writing in the *New York Herald-Tribune*, called the third act 'something of a miracle' but agreed that 'The rest of the play does not yet exist on the stage!' (3 May 1957, p. 12); the reviewer for *Theatre Arts* ranked the last forty-five minutes with the best of O'Neill (July 1957, pp. 12–13), while Henry Hewes in the *Saturday Review* more modestly judged that the 'flickering satisfactions' of the second half made attendance 'a rich and memorable experience' (18 May 1957, p. 34).

The critics were more united in praise of the acting: adjectives like 'magnificent', 'superb', and 'excellent' recur regularly. Although Wendy Hiller was not an obvious choice to play Josie, it had been recognised years before that the actor of the part need not be physically grotesque. Just as O'Neill had himself happily accepted Mary Welch in the part, so Harold Clurman had reported that Eva Dahlbeck, who in Stockholm had played Josie 'beautifully', did not match the playwright's description: Josie 'does not have to be "misbegotten" to believe she is undesirable; she needs only think of herself that way' (*Nation*, 8 May 1954, p. 409). Thus, Richard P. Cooke could call Hiller 'a good choice physically for the part . . ., sprawling all over the set one moment and the next giving us a portrait of a woman in love whose inner grace is as evident as her outer awkwardness'. Brooks Atkinson concurred that Hiller managed 'to look careless and brutish and at the same time radiate a kind of wistful glory', while Walter Kerr called her an 'image . . . you won't soon forget, or want to'. Only Henry Hewes complained that she worked 'frantically at contorting the face, walking in grotesque postures, and speaking in a slightly cockney accent' (Cooke confirmed that her 'British accent [came] through sometimes at wrong moments'). Franchot Tone also received excellent notices for his portrayal of Jim Tyrone, and the production achieved a modestly successful run of sixty-eight performances.

A Moon for the Misbegotten was next seen in New York in a production directed by Theodore Mann at the Circle in the Square; it opened on 12 June 1968 and had a popular run of 199 performances. Clive Barnes, writing in the *New York Times*, hailed the production as doing 'glorious justice' to a 'major minor-masterpiece' (13 June 1968, p. 55), a judgement of the play not echoed in other reviews. The critic for *Time* called it weak, 'more reverie than conflict, more dreams than drama', and yet responded to the 'poignant, subliminal dialogue that makes the audience hear what does not quite get said' (21 June 1968, p. 57). Henry Hewes, again reviewing the play for *Saturday Review* (29 June 1968, p. 40), gave it a rather grudging acceptance: while warning of the 'danger of boredom with O'Neill's constantly repeated technique of having a character say a line, negate it with an apology, and then berate himself with guilt for what he has said', he found that 'the geography of [the characters'] lives is somehow defined, and there is an exaltation in their coming to terms with its finality'. The cast, which included Salome Jens as Josie, Mitchell Ryan as Jim, and W.B. Brydon as Hogan, was generally praised by the critics and no doubt contributed to the play's success.

Considering the modest critical acclaim that greeted the 1968 revival, response to José Quintero's 1973 production at the Morosco Theater, New York, seems directed at a different play. Opening on 29 December with Colleen Dewhurst as Josie and Jason Robards Jr. as Jim, *A Moon for the Misbegotten* was now hailed by Clive Barnes as 'one of the 20th century's great plays' (*New York Times*, 31 December 1973, p. 22). While this change in perception may have been partly due to changing theatrical tastes, it was certainly helped by the involvement of the seasoned O'Neill director whose 1956 productions of *The Iceman Cometh* and *Long Day's Journey* had been responsible for the revival of interest in the playwright, as well as by the participation of the renowned O'Neill actor who had made his mark playing Hickey and Jamie in those same productions. Barnes called Quintero's *Moon for the Misbegotten* a 'landmark production' with an 'ideal, vibrant cast'. George Melloan, writing in the *Wall Street Journal* (2 January 1974, p. 6), agreed that this was a 'great production . . . almost magical in its ability to draw the audience close to the actors onstage in mood and feeling and close to O'Neill and his troubled psyche'. Play, acting, and production were equally praised: 'All the elements coalesce into something larger than the individual parts . . .'. The production had been planned for a limited run until 2 February but played for 313 performances.

A Moon for the Misbegotten was first seen in London on 20 January 1960 at the Arts Theatre in a production directed by Clifford Williams; Margaret Whiting, who had earlier distinguished herself in *The Iceman Cometh* at the Arts, played Josie, while Jim and Hogan were played respectively by Michael Aldridge and Colin Blakely. The play received mixed notices. Alan Pryce-Jones, writing for the *Observer*, called it 'a wonderful play' that contained O'Neill's 'characteristic faults and virtues': it was rather sentimental and needed tightening but 'refuse[d] to sag for long' – the 'steady tug towards a climax . . . held [the audience] all the way through', while much of the dialogue was 'briskly funny' (24 January 1960, p. 21). W.A. Darlington in the *Daily Telegraph* felt that the play gave 'glimpses of the author at his best – veiled and almost obscured by long passages in which his worst faults assert themselves'; his main complaints concerned the different mood of the play's two halves, a change for which the audience received no preparation, and the excessive repetition of the latter half (21 January 1960, p. 12).

Pryce-Jones praised the production's 'breath-catching modulations of acting' and greatly admired Whiting's performance, calling it 'the real thing: authority, tact and vision combined'; he also commented on the excellent support of Blakely and Aldridge. However, Harold Hobson in the *Sunday Times* (24 January 1960, p. 23) felt that the talk of Josie's size involved the audience in 'an unwilling . . . suspension of disbelief'; in his view, this contradiction between actual appearance and verbal description damaged the play, its 'uncomfortable values' vanishing along with the 'physical freak'. *The Times*'s reviewer straddled both sides of the fence, feeling that Whiting created the right grotesque impression during the play's first half and abandoned it in the second: she 'wears a pretty frock, cleans herself up, controls her hands politely, and . . . no longer appears quite the kind of heroine that the play requires'.

Such concerns about Josie's appearance did not arise when the play was revived at the Riverside Studios, Hammersmith, on 21 June 1983, in a production by David Leveaux, which later transferred to the Mermaid; Frances de la Tour played Josie, Alan Devlin Hogan, and Ian Bannen Jim, recreating the character he had portrayed in the first British production of *Long Day's Journey* in 1958. Although a few critics mentioned the mismatch between Josie's description and de la Tour's appearance, it was not considered significant: though 'physically nothing like' Josie, nevertheless de la Tour 'suggests in a glorious performance exactly the kind of woman Josie was' (B.A. Young, *Financial Times*). Milton Shulman commented that 'she beautifully builds . . . the aggressive shell protecting an inner softness' (*Standard*), while Ned Chaillet praised her 'gift of appearing ugly, both to herself and us, and of assuming rare beauty that is a little like having a peek at an angel's soul' (*Wall Street Journal*). These comments are representative of the general praise accorded the performances: Benedict Nightingale marvelled at 'the emotional resource, the concentration, the sheer *class*' of de la Tour and Bannen (*New Statesman*).

Reaction to the play itself varied. Giles Gordon recommended it to those who 'find the emotional confessions of uninteresting people interesting' (*Spectator*); Carole Woddis found it aroused not only compassion but irritation, as O'Neill pretends that Josie finds satisfaction in self-sacrifice (*City Limits*). Other commentators were much more positive: to Clive Hirschhorn the play revealed 'the very heart of the human condition' (*Sunday Express*), a judgement shared by several reviewers. Chaillet's verdict probably best sums up the play's potential as a superb vehicle for acting of the first rank: *A Moon for the Misbegotten* is 'a duct of shifting passions that is often genuinely poetic, and equally often genuinely raw and painful . . . . It is great writing, performed with a greatness of depth and understanding that is mesmerising.'

Christine Dymkowski
November 1991

Sources

Bogard, Travis and Jackson R. Breyer, eds. *Selected Letters of Eugene O'Neill*. New Haven and London: Yale University Press, 1988.

Cargill, Oscar, et al., eds. *O'Neill and His Plays: Four Decades of Criticism*. New York: New York University Press, 1961.

Floyd, Virginia, ed. *Eugene O'Neill at Work: Newly Released Ideas for Plays*. New York: Frederick Ungar, 1981.

Gelb, Arthur and Barbara. *O'Neill*. New York: Harper, 1960.

London Theatre Record (18 June–1 July 1983), pp. 485–87; (27 August–9 September 1983), p. 717, for reviews of the 1983 London production.

Miller, Jordan Y. *Eugene O'Neill and the American Critic: A Summary and Bibliographical Checklist*. Second edition, revised. Hamden, Connecticut: Archon, 1973.

Ranald, Margaret Loftus. *The Eugene O'Neill Companion*. Westport, Conn., and London: Greenwood, 1984.

Sheaffer, Louis. *O'Neill: Son and Playwright*. London: Dent, 1968.

──────────. *O'Neill: Son and Artist*. London: Paul Elek, 1973.

Welch, Mary. 'Softer Tones for Mr. O'Neill's Portrait', in Cargill, *O'Neill and His Plays*, pp. 85–91.

I would also like to thank Sue Cusworth of RHBNC for help in tracing British productions of O'Neill's plays.

List of O'Neill's Produced Plays

Title	Year Written*	First Production	First London Production
The Web	1913–14	39th Street Theatre, New York 17 March 1924	
Thirst	1913–14	Wharf Theatre, Provincetown, Mass. Summer 1916	
Fog	1913–14	Playwrights' Theater, New York 5 January 1917	
Bound East for Cardiff	1913–14	Wharf Theatre, Provincetown, Mass. 28 July 1916	(see S.S. Glencairn)
Servitude	1913–14	Skylark Theatre N.Y. International Airport 22 April 1960	
Abortion	1913–14	Key Theatre, New York 27 October 1959	
The Movie Man	1914	Key Theatre, New York 27 October 1959	

Title	Year Written*	First Production	First London Production
The Sniper	1915	Playwright's Theater, New York 16 February 1917	
Before Breakfast	1916	Playwrights' Theater, New York 1 December 1916	Gate Theatre 30 August 1926
Ile	1916–17	Playwrights' Theater, New York 30 November 1917	Everyman Theatre 17 April 1922
In the Zone	1916–17	Comedy Theater, New York (Washington Square Players) 31 October 1917	Everyman Theatre 15 June 1921
The Long Voyage Home	1916–17	Playwrights' Theater, New York 2 November 1917	Everyman Theatre 12 June 1925
The Moon of The Caribbees	1916–17	Playwrights' Theater, New York 20 December 1918	(see S.S. Glencairn)

S.S. Glencairn (*Bound East for Cardiff,* *In the Zone, Moon of the* *Caribbees,* and *Long* *Voyage Home*)		Barnstormer's Barn Provincetown, Massachusetts 14 August 1924	Mercury Theatre 9 June 1947
The Rope	1918	Playwrights' Theater, New York 26 April 1918	
The Dreamy Kid	1918	Playwrights' Theater, New York 31 October 1919	(Festival Theatre, Cambridge 14 May 1928)
Beyond the Horizon	1918	Morosco Theater, New York 3 February 1920	Regent Theatre (The Repertory Players) 31 January 1926
Where the Cross is Made	1918	Playwrights' Theater, New York 22 November 1918	Arts Theatre 27 October 1927
The Straw	1918–19	Greenwich Village Theater, New York 10 November 1921 (after an out-of-town tryout)	
Exorcism	1919	Playwrights' Theater, New York 26 March 1920	

Title	Year Written*	First Production	First London Production
Chris (1st version of *Anna Christie*)	1919	Apollo Theater, Atlantic City, N.J. 8 March 1920	
Gold	1920	Frazee Theater, New York 1 June 1921	
Anna Christie	1920	Vanderbilt Theater, New York 2 November 1921	Strand Theatre 10 April 1923
The Emperor Jones	1920	Playwrights' Theater, New York 1 November 1920	Ambassadors' Theatre 10 September 1925
Diff'rent	1920	Playwrights' Theater, New York 27 December 1920	Everyman Theatre 4 October 1921
The First Man	1921	Neighborhood Playhouse, New York 4 March 1922	
The Hairy Ape	1921	Playwrights' Theater, New York 9 March 1922	Gate Theatre 26 January 1928
The Fountain	1921–22	Greenwich Village Theater, New York 10 December 1925	

Welded	1922–23	39th Street Theater, New York 17 March 1924	The Playroom Six 16 February 1928
All God's Chillun Got Wings	1923	Provincetown Playhouse, New York 15 May 1924	Gate Theatre 8 November 1926
The Ancient Mariner (adaptation)	1924	Provincetown Playhouse (previously Playwrights' Theater), New York 6 April 1924	
Desire Under The Elms	1924	Greenwich Village Theater, New York 11 November 1924	Gate Theatre 24 February 1931
Marco Millions	1923–25	Guild Theater, New York 9 January 1928	Westminster Theatre 26 December 1938 (also produced at Festival Theatre, Cambridge, 1932)
The Great God Brown	1925	Greenwich Village Theater, New York 23 January 1926	Strand Theatre (Stage Society) 19 June 1927
Lazarus Laughed	1925–26	Pasadena Community Playhouse, California 9 April 1928	

Title	Year Written*	First Production	First London Production
Strange Interlude	1926–27	John Golden Theater, New York 30 January 1928	Lyric Theatre 3 February 1931
Dynamo	1928	Martin Beck Theater, New York 11 February 1929	
Mourning Becomes Electra	1929–31	Guild Theater, New York 26 October 1931	Westminster Theatre 19 November 1937
Ah! Wilderness	1932	Nixon Theater, Pittsburgh, Pennsylvania 25 September 1933 (out-of-town tryout before New York opening at Guild Theater, 2 October 1933)	Westminster Theatre 4 May 1936
Days Without End	1932–33	Plymouth Theater, Boston, Mass. 27 December 1933 (out-of-town tryout before New York opening at Guild Theater, 8 January 1934)	Grafton Theatre (Stage Society) 3 February 1935

A Touch of the Poet	1935–42	Royal Dramatic Theatre, Stockholm, Sweden 29 March 1957 (first American production at Helen Hayes Theater, New York, 2 October 1958)	Young Vic Theatre 20 January 1988 (also produced at Ashcroft Theatre, Croydon, 16 September 1963)
More Stately Mansions	1936–42	Royal Dramatic Theatre, Stockholm, Sweden 11 September 1962 (first American production at Ahmanson Theater, Los Angeles, California, 12 November 1967)	Greenwich Theatre 19 September 1974
The Iceman Cometh	1939	Martin Beck Theater, New York 9 October 1946	Arts Theatre 29 January 1958
Long Day's Journey into Night	1939–41	Royal Dramatic Theatre, Stockholm, Sweden 10 February 1956 (first American production at Helen Hayes Theater, New York, 7 November 1956)	Globe Theatre 24 September 1958 (transfer from Lyceum Theatre, Edinburgh, 8 September 1958)
Hughie	1941–42	Royal Dramatic Theatre, Stockholm, Sweden 18 September 1958	Duchess Theatre 18 June 1963
A Moon for the Misbegotten	1943	Hartman Theater, Columbus, Ohio (Guild Theater production) 20 February 1947	Arts Theatre 20 January 1960

*Dates of composition are approximate.

A MOON FOR THE MISBEGOTTEN

A Play in Four Acts

Characters

JOSIE HOGAN
PHIL HOGAN, her father
MIKE HOGAN, her brother
JAMES TYRONE, JR.
T. STEDMAN HARDER

Scenes

ACT ONE
The farmhouse. Around noon. Early September 1923.

ACT TWO
The same, but with the interior of sitting room revealed. Eleven
o'clock that night.

ACT THREE
The same as Act One. No time elapses between Acts Two and
Three.

ACT FOUR
The same. Dawn of the following morning.

General Scene

The play takes place in Connecticut at the home of tenant farmer Phil Hogan, between the hours of noon on a day in early September, 1923, and sunrise of the following day.

The house is not, to speak mildly, a fine example of New England architecture, placed so perfectly in its setting that it appears a harmonious part of the landscape, rooted in the earth. It has been moved to its present site, and looks it. An old box-like, clapboarded affair, with a shingled roof and brick chimney, it is propped up about two feet above ground by layers of timber blocks. There are two windows on the lower floor of this side of the house which faces front, and one window on the floor above. These windows have no shutters, curtains or shades. Each has at least one pane missing, a square of cardboard taking its place. The house had once been painted a repulsive yellow with brown trim, but the walls now are a blackened and weathered grey, flaked with streaks and splotches of dim lemon. Just around the left corner of the house, a flight of steps leads to the front door. To make matters worse, a one-storey, one-room addition has been tacked on at right. About twelve feet long by six high, this room, which is Josie Hogan's bedroom, is evidently home made. Its walls and sloping roof are covered with tar paper, faded to dark grey. Close to where it joins the house, there is a door with a flight of three unpainted steps leading to the ground. At right of door is a small window.

From these steps there is a footpath going around an old pear tree, at right-rear, through a field of hay stubble to a patch of woods. The same path also extends left to join a dirt road which leads up from the county highway (about a hundred yards off left) to the front door of the house, and thence back through a scraggly orchard of apple trees to the barn. Close to the house, under the window next to Josie's bedroom, there is a big boulder with a flat top.

ACT ONE

Scene. As described. It is just before noon. The day is clear and hot.

The door of JOSIE's *bedroom opens and she comes out on the steps, bending to avoid bumping her head.*

JOSIE *is twenty-eight. She is so oversize for a woman that she is almost a freak — five feet eleven in her stockings and weighs around one hundred and eighty. Her sloping shoulders are broad, her chest deep with large, firm breasts, her waist wide but slender by contrast with her hips and thighs. She has long arms, immensely strong, although no muscles show. The same is true of her legs.*

She is more powerful than any but an exceptionally strong man, able to do the manual labour of two ordinary men. But there is no mannish quality about her. She is all woman.

The map of Ireland is stamped on her face, with its long upper lip and small nose, thick black eyebrows, black hair as coarse as a horse's mane, freckled, sun-burned fair skin, high cheekbones and heavy jaw. It is not a pretty face, but her large dark-blue eyes give it a note of beauty, and her smile, revealing even white teeth, gives it charm.

She wears a cheap, sleeveless, blue cotton dress. Her feet are bare, the soles earth-stained and tough as leather.

She comes down the steps and goes left to the corner of the house and peers round it toward the barn. Then she moves swiftly to the right of the house and looks back.

JOSIE. Ah, thank God. (*She goes back toward the steps as her brother,* MIKE, *appears hurrying up from right-rear.*)

MIKE HOGAN *is twenty, about four inches shorter than his sister. He is sturdily built, but seems almost puny compared to her. He has a common Irish face, its expression sullen, or slyly cunning, or primly self-righteous. He never forgets that he is a good Catholic, faithful to all the observances, and so is one of the élite of Almighty God in a world of damned sinners composed of Protestants and bad Catholics. In brief,* MIKE *is a New England Irish Catholic Puritan, Grade B, and an extremely irritating youth to have around.*

MIKE *wears dirty overalls, a sweat-stained brown shirt. He carries a pitchfork.*

JOSIE. Bad luck to you for a slowpoke. Didn't I tell you half-past eleven?

MIKE. How could I sneak here sooner with him peeking round the corner of the barn to catch me if I took a minute's rest, the way he always does? I had to wait till he went to the pigpen. (*He adds viciously.*) Where he belongs, the old hog!

JOSIE's *right arm strikes with surprising swiftness and her big hand lands on the side of his jaw. She means it to be only a slap, but his head jerks back and he stumbles, dropping the pitchfork, and pleads cringingly.*

Don't hit me, Josie! Don't, now!

JOSIE (*quietly*). Then keep your tongue off him. He's my father, too, and I like him, if you don't.

MIKE (*out of reach – sullenly*). You're two of a kind, and a bad kind.

JOSIE (*good-naturedly*). I'm proud of it. And I didn't hit you, or you'd be flat on the ground. It was only a love tap to waken your wits, so you'll use them. If he catches you running away, he'll beat you half to death. Get your bag now. I've packed it. It's inside the door of my room with your coat laid over it. Hurry now, while I see what he's doing.

She moves quickly to peer around the corner of the house at left. He goes up the steps into her room and returns carrying an old coat and a cheap bulging satchel. She comes back.

There's no sight of him.

MIKE *drops the satchel on the ground while he puts on the coat.*

I put everything in the bag. You can change to your Sunday suit in the can at the station or in the train, and don't forget to wash your face. I know you want to look your best when our brother, Thomas, sees you on his doorstep. (*Her tone becomes derisively amused.*) And him way up in the world, a noble sergeant of the Bridgeport police. Maybe he'll get you on the force. It'd suit you. I can see you leading drunks to the lockup while you give them a lecture on temperance. Or if Thomas can't get you a job, he'll pass you along to our brother, John, the noble bar-keep in Meriden. He'll teach you the trade. You'll make a nice one, who'll never steal from the till, or drink, and who'll tell customers they've had enough and better go home just when they're beginning to feel happy. (*She sighs regretfully.*)

Ah, well, Mike, you was born a priest's pet, and there's no help for it.

MIKE. That's right! Make fun of me again, because I want to be decent.

JOSIE. You're worse than decent. You're virtuous.

MIKE. Well, that's a thing nobody can say about – (*He stops, a bit ashamed, but mostly afraid to finish.*)

JOSIE (*amused*). About me? No, and what's more, they don't. (*She smiles mockingly.*) I know what a trial it's been to you, Mike, having a sister who's the scandal of the neighbourhood.

MIKE. It's you that's saying it, not me. I don't want to part with hard feelings. And I'll keep on praying for you.

JOSIE (*roughly*). Och! To hell with your prayers!

MIKE (*stiffly*). I'm going. (*He picks up his bag.*)

JOSIE (*her manner softening*). Wait. (*She comes to him.*) Don't mind my rough tongue, Mike. I'm sorry to see you go, but it's the best thing for you. That's why I'm helping you, the same as I helped Thomas and John. You can't stand up to the Old Man any more than Thomas or John could, and the old divil would always keep you a slave. I wish you all the luck in the world, Mike. I know you'll get on – and God bless you. (*Her voice has softened, and she blinks back tears. She kisses him – then fumbling in the pocket of her dress, pulls out a little roll of one-dollar bills and presses it in his hand.*) Here's a little present over your fare. I took it from his little green bag, and won't he be wild when he finds out! But I can handle him.

MIKE (*enviously*). You can. You're the only one. (*Gratefully moved for a second.*) Thank you, Josie. You've a kind heart. (*Then virtuously.*) But I don't like taking stolen money.

JOSIE. Don't be a bigger jackass than you are already. Tell your conscience it's a bit of the wages he's never given you.

MIKE. That's true, Josie. It's rightfully mine. (*He shoves the money into his pocket.*)

JOSIE. Get along now, so you won't miss the trolley. And don't forget to get off the train at Bridgeport. Give my love to Thomas and John. No, never mind. They've not written me in years. Give them a boot in the tail for me.

MIKE. That's nice talk for a woman. You've a tongue as dirty as the Old Man's.

JOSIE (*impatiently*). Don't start preaching, like you love to, or you'll never go.

MIKE. You're as bad as he is, almost. It's his influence made you what you are, and him always scheming how he'll cheat people, selling them a broken-down nag or a sick cow or pig that he's doctored up to look good for a day or two. It's no better than stealing, and you help him.

JOSIE. I do. Sure, it's grand fun.

MIKE. You ought to marry and have a home of your own away from this shanty and stop your shameless ways with men. (*He adds, not without moral satisfaction.*) Though it'd be hard to find a decent man who'd have you now.

JOSIE. I don't want a decent man, thank you. They're no fun. They're all sticks like you. And I wouldn't marry the best man on earth and be tied down to him alone.

MIKE (*with a cunning leer*). Not even Jim Tyrone, I suppose? (*She stares at him.*) You'd like being tied to money, I know that, and he'll be rich when his mother's estate is settled. (*Sarcastically.*) I suppose you've never thought of that? Don't tell me! I've watched you making sheep's eyes at him.

JOSIE (*contemptuously*). So I'm leading Jim on to propose, am I?

MIKE. I know it's crazy, but maybe you're hoping if you got hold of him alone when he's mad drunk – Anyway, talk all you please to put me off, I'll bet my last penny you've cooked up some scheme to hook him, and the Old Man put you up to it. Maybe he thinks if he caught you with Jim and had witnesses to prove it, and his shotgun to scare him –

JOSIE (*controlling her anger*). You're full of bright thoughts. I wouldn't strain my brains any more, if I was you.

MIKE. Well, I wouldn't put it past the Old Man to try any trick. And I wouldn't put it past you, God forgive you. You've never cared about your virtue, or what man you went out with. You've always been brazen as brass and proud of your disgrace. You can't deny that, Josie.

JOSIE. I don't. (*Then ominously.*) You'd better shut up now. I've been holding my temper, because we're saying goodbye. (*She stands up.*) But I'm losing patience.

MIKE (*hastily*). Wait till I finish and you won't be mad at me. I was going to say I wish you luck with your scheming, for once. I hate Jim Tyrone's guts, with his quotin' Latin and his high-toned Jesuit College education, putting on airs as if he was too good to wipe his shoes on me, when he's nothing but a drunken bum who never done a tap of work in his life, except acting on the stage while his father was alive to get him the jobs. (*Vindictively.*) I'll pray you'll find a way to nab him, Josie, and skin him out of his last nickel!

JOSIE (*makes a threatening move toward him*). One more word out of you – (*Then contemptuously.*) You're a dirty tick and it'd serve you right if I let you stay gabbing until Father came and beat you to a jelly, but I won't. I'm too anxious to be rid of you. (*Roughly.*) Get out of here, now! Do you think he'll stay all day with the pigs, you gabbing fool? (*She goes left to peer around the corner of the house – with real alarm.*) There he is, coming up to the barn.

MIKE *grabs the satchel, terrified. He slinks swiftly around the corner and disappears along the path to the woods, right-rear. She keeps watching her father and does not notice* MIKE's *departure.*

He's looking toward the meadow. He sees you're not working. He's running down there. He'll come here next. You'd better run for your life! (*She turns and sees he's gone – contemptuously.*) I might have known. I'll bet you're a mile away by now, you rabbit! (*She peeks around the corner again – with amused admiration.*) Look at my poor old father pelt. He's as spry on his stumpy legs as a yearling – and as full of rage as a nest of wasps! (*She laughs and comes back to look along the path to the woods.*) Well, that's the last of you, Mike, and good riddance. It was the little boy you used to be that I had to mother, and not you, I stole the money for. (*This dismisses him. She sighs.*) Well, himself will be here in a minute. I'd better be ready. (*She reaches in her bedroom corner by the door and takes out a sawed-off broom handle.*) Not that I need it, but it saves his pride. (*She sits on the steps with the broom handle propped against the steps near her right hand.*)

A moment later, her father, PHIL HOGAN, *comes running up from left-rear and charges around the corner of the house, his arms pumping up and down, his fists clenched, his face full of fighting fury.*

HOGAN *is fifty-five, about five feet six. He has a thick neck, lumpy, sloping shoulders, a barrel-like trunk, stumpy legs, and big feet. His arms are short and muscular, with large hairy hands. His head is round with thinning sandy hair. His face is fat with a snub nose, long upper lip, big mouth, and little blue eyes with bleached lashes and eyebrows that remind one of a white pig's. He wears heavy brogans, filthy overalls, and a dirty short-sleeved undershirt. Arms and face are sunburned and freckled. On his head is an old wide-brimmed hat of coarse straw that would look more becoming on a horse. His voice is high-pitched with a pronounced brogue.*

HOGAN (*stops as he turns the corner and sees her – furiously*). Where is he? Is he hiding in the house? I'll wipe the floors with him, the lazy bastard! (*Turning his anger against her.*) Haven't you a tongue in your head, you great slut you?

JOSIE (*with provoking calm*). Don't be calling me names, you bad-tempered old hornet, or maybe I'll lose my temper, too.

HOGAN. To hell with your temper, you overgrown cow!

JOSIE. I'd rather be a cow than an ugly little buck goat. You'd better sit down and cool off. Old men shouldn't run around raging in the noon sun. You'll get sunstroke.

HOGAN. To hell with sunstroke! Have you seen him?

JOSIE. Have I seen who?

HOGAN. Mike! Who else would I be after, the Pope? He was in the meadow, but the minute I turned my back he sneaked off. (*He sees the pitchfork.*) There's his pitchfork! Will you stop your lying!

JOSIE. I haven't said I didn't see him.

HOGAN. Then don't try to help him hide from me, or – Where is he?

JOSIE. Where you'll never find him.

HOGAN. We'll soon see! I'll bet he's in your room under the bed, the cowardly lump! (*He moves toward the steps.*)

JOSIE. He's not. He's gone like Thomas and John before him to escape your slave-driving.

HOGAN (*stares at her incredulously*). You mean he's run off to make his own way in the world?

JOSIE. He has. So make up your mind to it, and sit down.

HOGAN (*baffled, sits on the boulder and takes off his hat to scratch his head – with a faint trace of grudging respect*). I'd never dream he had that much spunk. (*His temper rising again.*) And I know damned well he hadn't, not without you to give him the guts and help him, like the great soft fool you are!

JOSIE. Now don't start raging again, Father.

HOGAN (*seething*). You've stolen my satchel to give him, I suppose, like you did before for Thomas and John?

JOSIE. It was my satchel, too. Didn't I help you in the trade for the horse, when you got the Crowleys to throw in the satchel for good measure? I was up all night fixing that nag's forelegs so his knees wouldn't buckle together till after the Crowleys had him a day or two.

HOGAN (*forgets his anger to grin reminiscently*). You've a wonderful way with animals, God bless you. And do you remember the two Crowleys came back to give me a beating, and I licked them both?

JOSIE (*with calculating flattery*). You did. You're a wonderful fighter. Sure, you could give Jack Dempsey himself a run for his money.

HOGAN (*with sharp suspicion*). I could, but don't try to change the subject and fill me with blarney.

JOSIE. All right. I'll tell the truth then. They were getting the best of you till I ran out and knocked one of them tail over tin cup against the pigpen.

HOGAN (*outraged*). You're a liar! They was begging for mercy before you came. (*Furiously.*) You thief, you! You stole my fine satchel for that lump! And I'll bet that's not all. I'll bet, like when Thomas and John sneaked off, you – (*He rises from the boulder threateningly.*) Listen, Josie, if you found where I hid my little green bag, and stole my money to give to that lousy altar boy, I'll –

JOSIE (*rises from the steps with the broom handle in her right hand*). Well, I did. So now what'll you do? Don't be threatening me. You know I'll beat better sense in your skull if you lay a finger on me.

HOGAN. I never yet laid hands on a woman – not when I was sober – but if it wasn't for that club – (*Bitterly.*) A fine curse God put on me when he gave me a daughter as big and strong as a bull, and as vicious and disrespectful. (*Suddenly his eyes twinkle and he grins admiringly.*) Be God, look at you standing there with the club! If you ain't the damnedest daughter in Connecticut, who is? (*He chuckles and sits on the boulder again.*)

JOSIE (*laughs and sits on the steps, putting the club away*). And if you ain't the damnedest father in Connecticut, who is?

HOGAN (*takes a clay pipe and plug of tobacco and knife from his pocket. He cuts the plug and stuffs his pipe – without rancour*). How much did you steal, Josie?

JOSIE. Six dollars only.

HOGAN. *Only!* Well, God grant someone with wits will see that dopey gander at the depot and sell him the railroad for the six. (*Grumbling.*) It isn't the money I mind, Josie –

JOSIE. I know. Sure, what do you care for money? You'd give your last penny to the first beggar you met – if he had a shotgun pointed at your heart!

HOGAN. Don't be teasing. You know what I mean. It's the thought of that pious lump having my money that maddens me. I wouldn't put it past him to drop it in the collection plate next Sunday, he's that big a jackass.

JOSIE. I knew when you'd calmed down you'd think it worth six dollars to see the last of him.

HOGAN (*finishes filling his pipe*). Well, maybe I do. To tell the truth, I never liked him. (*He strikes a match on the seat of his overalls and lights his pipe.*) And I never liked Thomas and John, either.

JOSIE (*amused*). You've the same bad luck in sons I have in brothers.

HOGAN (*puffs ruminatively*). They all take after your mother's family. She was the only one in it had spirit, God rest her soul. The rest of them was a pious lot. They wouldn't dare put food in their mouths before they said grace for it. They was too busy preaching temperance to have time for a drink. They spent so much time confessing their sins, they had no chance to do any sinning. (*He spits disgustedly.*) The scum of the earth! Thank God, you're like me and your mother.

JOSIE. I don't know if I should thank God for being like you. Sure, everyone says you're a wicked old tick, as crooked as a corkscrew.

HOGAN. I know. They're an envious lot, God forgive them.

(*They both chuckle. He pulls on his pipe reflectively.*) You didn't get much thanks from Mike, I'll wager, for your help.

JOSIE. Oh, he thanked me kindly. And then he started to preach about my sins – and yours.

HOGAN. Oho, did he? (*Exploding.*) For the love of God, why didn't you hold him till I could give him one good kick for a father's parting blessing!

JOSIE. I near gave him one myself.

HOGAN. When I think your poor mother was killed bringing that crummy calf into life! (*Vindictively.*) I've never set foot in a church since, and never will. (*A pause. He speaks with a surprising sad gentleness.*) A sweet woman. Do you remember her, Josie? You were only a little thing when she died.

JOSIE. I remember her well. (*With a teasing smile which is half sad.*) She was the one could put you in your place when you'd come home drunk and want to tear down the house for the fun of it.

HOGAN (*with admiring appreciation*). Yes, she could do it, God bless her. I only raised my hand to her once – just a slap because she told me to stop singing, it was after daylight. The next moment I was on the floor thinking a mule had kicked me. (*He chuckles.*) Since you've grown up, I've had the same trouble. There's no liberty in my own home.

JOSIE. That's lucky – or there wouldn't be any home.

HOGAN (*after a pause of puffing on his pipe*). What did that donkey, Mike, preach to you about?

JOSIE. Oh, the same as ever – that I'm the scandal of the countryside, carrying on with men without a marriage licence.

HOGAN (*gives her a strange, embarrassed glance and then looks away. He does not look at her during the following dialogue. His manner is casual*). Hell roast his soul for saying it. But it's true enough.

JOSIE (*defiantly*). It is, and what of it? I don't care a damn for the scandal.

HOGAN. No. You do as you please and to hell with everyone.

JOSIE. Yes, and that goes for you, too, if you are my father. So don't you start preaching too.

HOGAN. Me, preach? Sure, the divil would die laughing. Don't bring me into it. I learned long since to let you go your own way because there's no controlling you.

JOSIE. I do my work and I earn my keep and I've a right to be free.

HOGAN. You have. I've never denied it.

JOSIE. No. You've never. I've often wondered why a man that likes fights as much as you didn't grab at the excuse of my disgrace to beat the lights out of the men.

HOGAN. Wouldn't I look a great fool, when everyone knows any man who tried to make free with you, and you not willing, would be carried off to the hospital? Anyway, I wouldn't want to fight an army. You've had too many sweethearts.

JOSIE (*with a proud toss of her head – boastfully*). That's because I soon get tired of any man and give him his walking papers.

HOGAN. I'm afraid you were born to be a terrible wanton woman. But to tell the truth, I'm well satisfied you're what you are, though I shouldn't say it, because if you was the decent kind you'd have married some fool long ago, and I'd have lost your company and your help on the farm.

JOSIE (*with a trace of bitterness*). Leave it to you to think of your own interest.

HOGAN (*puffs on his pipe*). What else did my beautiful son, Mike, say to you?

JOSIE. Oh, he was full of stupid gab, as usual. He gave me good advice –

HOGAN (*grimly*). That was kind of him. It must have been good –

JOSIE. I ought to marry and settle down – if I could find a decent man who'd have me, which he was sure I couldn't.

HOGAN (*beginning to boil*). I tell you, Josie, it's going to be the saddest memory of my life I didn't get one last swipe at him!

JOSIE. So the only hope he thought, was for me to catch some indecent man, who'd have money coming to him I could steal.

HOGAN (*gives her a quick, probing side glance – casually*). He meant Jim Tyrone?

JOSIE. He did. And the dirty tick accused you and me of making up a foxy scheme to trap Jim. I'm to get him alone when he's crazy drunk and lead him on to marry me. (*She adds in a hard, scornful tone.*) As if that would ever work. Sure, all the pretty little tarts on Broadway, New York, must have had a try at that, and much good it did them.

HOGAN (*again with a quick side glance – casually*). They must have, surely. But that's in the city where he's suspicious. You can never tell what he mightn't do here in the country, where he's innocent, with a moon in the sky to fill him with poetry and a quart of bad hooch inside of him.

JOSIE (*turns on him angrily*). Are you taking Mike's scheme seriously, you old goat?

HOGAN. I'm not. I only thought you wanted my opinion. (*She regards him suspiciously, but his face is blank as if he hadn't a thought beyond enjoying his pipe.*)

JOSIE (*turning away*). And if that didn't work, Mike said maybe we had a scheme that I'd get Jim in bed with me and you'd come with witnesses and a shotgun, and catch him there.

HOGAN. Faith, me darlin' son never learnt that from his prayer book! He must have improved his mind on the sly.

JOSIE. The dirty tick!

HOGAN. Don't call him a tick. I don't like ticks but I'll say this for them, I never picked one off me yet was a hypocrite.

JOSIE. Him daring to accuse us of planning a rotten trick like that on Jim!

HOGAN (*as if he misunderstood her meaning*). Yes, it's as old as the hills. Everyone's heard of it. But it still works now and again, I'm told, and sometimes an old trick is best because it's so ancient no one would suspect you'd try it.

JOSIE (*staring at him resentfully*). That's enough out of you, Father. I never can tell to this day, when you put that dead mug on you, whether you're joking or not, but I don't want to hear any more –

HOGAN (*mildly*). I thought you wanted my honest opinion on the merits of Mike's suggestion.

JOSIE. Och, shut up, will you? I know you're only trying to make game of me. You like Jim and you'd never play a dirty trick on him, not even if I was willing.

HOGAN. No – not unless I found he was playing one on me.

JOSIE. Which he'd never.

HOGAN. No, I wouldn't think it, but my motto in life is never trust anyone too far, not even myself.

JOSIE. You've reason for the last. I've often suspected you sneak out of bed in the night and pick your own pockets.

HOGAN. I wouldn't call it a dirty trick on him to get you for a wife.

JOSIE (*exasperatedly*). God save us, are you off on that again?

HOGAN. Well, you've put marriage in my head and I can't help considering the merits of the case, as they say. Sure, you're two of a kind, both great disgraces. That would help make a happy marriage because neither of you could look down on the other.

JOSIE. Jim mightn't think so.

HOGAN. You mean he'd think he was marrying beneath his station? He'd be a damned fool if he had that notion, for his Old Man who'd worked up from nothing to be rich and famous didn't give a damn about station. Didn't I often see him working on his grounds in clothes I wouldn't put on a scarecrow, not caring who saw him? (*With admiring affection.*) God rest him, he was a true Irish gentleman.

JOSIE. He was, and didn't you swindle him, and make me help you at it? I remember when I was a slip of a girl, and you'd get a letter saying his agent told him you were a year behind in the rent, and he'd be damned if he'd stand for it, and he was coming here to settle the matter. You'd make me dress up, with my hair brushed and a ribbon in it, and leave me to soften his heart before he saw you. So I'd skip down the path to meet him, and make him a curtsey, and hold on to his hand, and bat my eyes at him and lead him in the house, and offer him a drink of the good whiskey you didn't keep for company, and gape at him and tell him he was the handsomest man in the world, and the fierce expression he'd put on for you would go away.

HOGAN (*chuckles*). You did it wonderful. You should have gone on the stage.

JOSIE (*dryly*). Yes, that's what he'd tell me, and he'd reach in his pocket and take out a half dollar, and ask me if you hadn't put me up to it. So I'd say yes, you had.

HOGAN (*sadly*). I never knew you were such a black traitor, and you only a child.

JOSIE. And then you'd come and before he could get a word out of him, you'd tell him you'd vacate the premises unless he lowered the rent and painted the house.

HOGAN. Be God, that used to stop him in his tracks.

JOSIE. It didn't stop him from saying you were the damnedest crook ever came out of Ireland.

HOGAN. He said it with admiration. And we'd start drinking and telling stories, and singing songs, and by the time he left we were both too busy cursing England to worry over the rent. (*He grins affectionately.*) Oh, he was a great man entirely.

JOSIE. He was. He always saw through your tricks.

HOGAN. Didn't I know he would? Sure, all I wanted was to give him the fun of seeing through them so he couldn't be hard-hearted. That was the real trick.

JOSIE (*stares at him*). You old divil, you've always a trick hidden behind your tricks, so no one can tell at times what you're after.

HOGAN. Don't be so suspicious. Sure, I'd never try to fool you. You know me too well. But we've gone off the track. It's Jim we're discussing, not his father. I was telling you I could see the merit in your marrying him.

JOSIE (*exasperatedly*). Och, a cow must have kicked you in the head this morning.

HOGAN. I'd never give it a thought if I didn't know you had a soft spot in your heart for him.

JOSIE (*resentfully*). Well, I haven't! I like him, if that's what you mean, but it's only to talk to, because he's educated and quiet-spoken and has politeness even when he's drunkest, and doesn't roar around cursing and singing like some I could name.

HOGAN. If you could see the light in your eyes when he blarneys you –

JOSIE (*roughly*). The light in me foot! (*Scornfully.*) I'm in love with him, you'll be saying next!

HOGAN (*ignores this*). And another merit of the case is, he likes you.

JOSIE. Because he keeps dropping in here lately? Sure, it's only when he gets sick of the drunks at the Inn, and it's more to joke with you than see me.

HOGAN. It's your happiness I'm considering when I recommend your using your wits to catch him, if you can.

JOSIE (*jeeringly*). If!

HOGAN. Who knows? With all the sweethearts you've had, you must have a catching way with men.

JOSIE (*boastfully*). Maybe I have. But that doesn't mean –

HOGAN. If you got him alone tonight – there'll be a beautiful moon to fill him with poetry and loneliness, and –

JOSIE. That's one of Mike's dirty schemes.

HOGAN. Mike be damned! Sure, that's every woman's scheme since the world was created. Without it there'd be no population. (*Persuasively.*) There'd be no harm trying it, anyway.

JOSIE. And no use, either. (*Bitterly.*) Och, Father, don't play the jackass with me. You know, and I know, I'm an ugly overgrown lump of a woman, and the men that want me are no better than stupid bulls. Jim can have all the pretty, painted little Broadway girls he wants – and dancers on the stage, too – when he comes into his estate. That's the kind he likes.

HOGAN. I notice he's never married one. Maybe he'd like a fine strong handsome figure of a woman for a change, with beautiful eyes and hair and teeth and a smile.

JOSIE (*pleased, but jeering*). Thank you kindly for your compliments. Now I know a cow kicked you in the head.

HOGAN. If you think Jim hasn't been taking in your fine points, you're a fool.

JOSIE. You mean you've noticed him? (*Suddenly furious.*) Stop your lying!

HOGAN. Don't fly in a temper. All I'm saying is, there may be a chance in it to better yourself.

JOSIE (*scornfully*). Better myself by being tied down to a man who's drunk every night of his life? No, thank you!

HOGAN. Sure, you're strong enough to reform him. A taste of that club you've got, when he came home to you paralysed, and in a few weeks you'd have him a dirty prohibitionist.

JOSIE (*seriously*). It's true, if I was his wife, I'd cure him of drinking himself to death, if I had to kill him. (*Then angrily.*) Och, I'm sick of your crazy gab, Father! Leave me alone!

HOGAN. Well, let's put it another way. Don't tell me you couldn't learn to love the estate he'll come into.

JOSIE (*resentfully*). Ah, I've been waiting for that. That's what Mike said, again. Now we've come to the truth behind all your blather of my liking him or him liking me. (*Her manner changing – defiantly.*) All right, then. Of course I'd love the money. Who wouldn't? And why shouldn't I get my hands on it, if I could? He's bound to be swindled out of it, anyway. He'll go back to the Broadway he thinks is heaven, and by the time the pretty little tarts, and the bar-room sponges and race-track touts and gamblers are through with him he'll be picked clean. I'm no saint, God knows, but I'm decent and deserving compared to those scum.

HOGAN (*eagerly*). Be God, now you're using your wits. And where there's a will there's a way. You and me have never been beat when we put our brains together. I'll keep thinking it over, and you do the same.

JOSIE (*with illogical anger*). Well, I won't! And you keep your mad scheming to yourself. I won't listen to it.

HOGAN (*as if he were angry, too*). All right. The divil take you. It's all you'll hear from me. (*He pauses – then with great seriousness, turning toward her.*) Except one thing – (*As she starts to shut him up – sharply.*) I'm serious, and you'd better listen, because it's about this farm, which is home to us.

JOSIE (*surprised, stares at him*). What about the farm?

HOGAN. Don't forget, if we have lived on it twenty years, we're only tenants and we could be thrown out on our necks any-time. (*Quickly.*) Mind you, I don't say Jim would ever do it, rent or no rent, or let the executors do it, even if they wanted, which they don't, knowing they'd never find another tenant.

JOSIE. What's worrying you, then?

HOGAN. This. I've been afraid lately the minute the estate is out of probate, Jim will sell the farm.

JOSIE (*exasperatedly*). Of course he will! Hasn't he told us and promised you can buy it on easy time payments at the small price you offered?

HOGAN. Jim promises whatever you like when he's full of whiskey. He might forget a promise as easy when he's drunk enough.

JOSIE (*indignantly*). He'd never! And who'd want it except us? No one ever has in all the years –

HOGAN. Someone has lately. The agent got an offer last month, Jim told me, bigger than mine.

JOSIE. Och, Jim loves to try and get your goat. He was kidding you.

HOGAN. He wasn't. I can tell. He said he told the agent to tell whoever it was the place wasn't for sale.

JOSIE. Of course he did. Did he say who'd made the offer?

HOGAN. He didn't know. It came through a real-estate man who wouldn't tell who his client was. I've been trying to guess, but I can't think of anyone crazy enough unless it'd be some damn fool of a millionaire buying up land to make a great estate for himself, like our beautiful neighbour, Harder, the Standard Oil thief, did years ago. (*He adds with bitter fervency.*) May he roast in hell and his Limey superintendent with him!

JOSIE. Amen to that. (*Then scornfully.*) This land for an estate? And if there was an offer, Jim's refused it, and that ends it. He wouldn't listen to any offer, after he's given his word to us.

HOGAN. Did I say he would – when he's in his right mind? What I'm afraid of is, he might be led into it sometime when he has one of his sneering bitter drunks on and talks like a Broadway crook himself, saying money is the only thing in the world, and everything and anyone can be bought if the price is big enough. You've heard him.

JOSIE. I have. But he doesn't fool me at all. He only acts like he's hard and shameless to get back at life when it's tormenting him – and who doesn't?

He gives her a quick, curious side glance which she doesn't notice.

HOGAN. Or take the other kind of queer drunk he gets on sometimes when, without any reason you can see, he'll suddenly turn strange, and look sad, and stare at nothing as if he was mourning over some ghost inside him, and –

JOSIE. I think I know what comes over him when he's like that. It's the memory of his poor mother comes back and his grief for her death. (*Pityingly.*) Poor Jim.

HOGAN (*ignoring this*). And whiskey seems to have no effect on him, like water off a duck's back. He'll keep acting natural enough, and you'd swear he wasn't bad at all, but the next day you find his brain was so paralysed he don't remember a thing until you remind him. He's done a lot of mad things, when he was that way, he was sorry for after.

JOSIE (*scornfully*). What drunk hasn't? But he'd never – (*Resentfully.*) I won't have you suspecting Jim without any cause, d'you hear me!

HOGAN. I don't suspect him. All I've said is, when a man gets as queer drunk as Jim, he doesn't know himself what he mightn't do, and we'd be damned fools if we didn't fear the possibility, however small it is, and do all we can to guard against it.

JOSIE. There's no possibility! And how could we guard against it, if there was?

HOGAN. Well, you can put yourself out to be extra nice to him, for one thing.

JOSIE. How nice is extra nice!

HOGAN. You ought to know. But here's one tip. I've noticed when you talk rough and brazen like you do to other men, he may grin like they do, as if he enjoyed it, but he don't. So watch your tongue.

JOSIE (*with a defiant toss of her head*). I'll talk as I please, and if he don't like it he can lump it! (*Scornfully.*) I'm to pretend I'm a pure virgin, I suppose? That would fool him, wouldn't it, and him hearing all about me from the men at the Inn? (*She gets to her feet, abruptly changing the subject.*) We're wasting the day, blathering. (*Then her face hardening.*) If ever he went back on his word, no matter how drunk he was, I'd be with you in any scheme you made against him, no matter how dirty. (*Hastily.*) But it's all your nonsense. I'd never believe it. (*She comes and picks up the pitchfork.*) I'll go to the meadow and finish Mike's work. You needn't fear you'll miss his help on the farm.

HOGAN. A hell of a help! A weak lazy back and the appetite of a drove of starving pigs! (*As she turns to go – suddenly bellicose.*) Leaving me, are you? When it's dinner time? Where's my dinner, you lazy cow?

JOSIE. There's stew on the stove, you bad-tempered runt. Go in and help yourself. I'm not hungry. Your gab has bothered my mind. I need hard work in the sun to clear it. (*She starts to go off toward rear-right.*)

HOGAN (*glancing down the road, off left-front*). You'd better wait. There's a caller coming to the gate – and if I'm not mistaken, it's the light of your eyes himself.

JOSIE (*angrily*). Shut up! (*She stares off – her face softens and grows pitying.*) Look at him when he thinks no one is watching, with his eyes on the ground. Like a dead man walking slow behind his own coffin. (*Then roughly.*) Faith, he must have a hangover. He sees us now. Look at the bluff he puts up, straightening himself and grinning. (*Resentfully.*) I don't want to meet him. Let him make jokes with you and play the old game about a drink you both think is such fun. That's all he comes for, anyway. (*She starts off again.*)

HOGAN. Are you running away from him? Sure, you must be afraid you're in love.

JOSIE *halts instantly and turns back defiantly.*

(*He goes on.*) Go in the house now and wash your face, and tidy your dress, and give a touch to your hair. You want to look decent for him.

JOSIE (*angrily*). I'll go in the house, but only to see the stew ain't burned, for I suppose you'll have the foxiness to ask him to have a bite to eat to keep in his good graces.

HOGAN. Why shouldn't I ask him? I know damned well he has no appetite this early in the day, but only a thirst.

JOSIE. Och, you make me sick, you sly miser! (*She goes in through her bedroom, slamming the door behind her.*)

HOGAN *refills his pipe, pretending he doesn't notice* TYRONE *approaching, his eyes bright with droll expectation.* JIM TYRONE *enters along the road from the highway, left.*

TYRONE *is in his early forties, around five feet nine, broad-shouldered and deep-chested. His naturally fine physique has become soft and soggy from dissipation, but his face is still good-looking despite its unhealthy puffiness and the bags under the eyes. He has thinning dark hair, parted and brushed back to cover a bald spot. His eyes are brown, the whites congested and yellowish. His nose, big and aquiline, gives his face a certain Mephistophelian quality which is accentuated by his habitually cynical expression. But when he smiles without sneering, he still has the ghost of a former youthful, irresponsible Irish charm – that of the beguiling ne'er-do-well, sentimental and romantic. It is his humour and charm which have kept him attractive to women, and popular with men as a drinking companion. He is dressed in an expensive dark-brown suit, tight-fitting and drawn in at the waist, dark brown made-to-order shoes and silk socks, a white silk shirt, silk handkerchief in breast pocket, a dark tie. This get-up suggests that he follows a style set by well-groomed Broadway gamblers who would like to be mistaken for Wall Street brokers.*

He has had enough pick-me-ups to recover from morning-after nausea and steady his nerves. During the following dialogue, he and HOGAN are like players at an old familiar game where each knows the other's moves, but which still amuses them.

TYRONE (*approaches and stands regarding* HOGAN *with sardonic relish.* HOGAN *scratches a match on the seat of his overalls and lights his pipe, pretending not to see him.* TYRONE *recites with feeling*).

Fortunate senex, ergo tua rura manebunt,
et tibi magna satis, quamvis lapis omnia nudus.

HOGAN (*mutters*). It's the landlord again, and my shotgun not handy. (*He looks up at* TYRONE.) Is it Mass you're saying, Jim? That was Latin. I know it by ear. What the hell – insult does it mean?

TYRONE. Translated very freely into Irish English, something like this. (*He imitates* HOGAN's *brogue*.) 'Ain't you the lucky old bastard to have this beautiful farm, if it is full of nude rocks.'

HOGAN. I like that part about the rocks. If cows could eat them this place would make a grand dairy farm. (*He spits.*) It's easy to see you've a fine college education. It must be a big help to you, conversing with whores and bar-keeps.

TYRONE. Yes, a very worldly asset. I was once offered a job as office boy – until they discovered I wasn't qualified because I had no Bachelor of Arts diploma. There had been a slight misunderstanding just before I was to graduate.

HOGAN. Between you and the Fathers? I'll wager!

TYRONE. I made a bet with another Senior I could get a tart from Haymarket to visit me, introduce her to the Jebs as my sister – and get away with it.

HOGAN. But you didn't?

TYRONE. Almost. It was a memorable day in the halls of learning. All the students were wise and I had them rolling in the aisles as I showed Sister around the grounds, accompanied by one of the Jebs. He was a bit suspicious at first, but Dutch

Maisie – her professional name – had no make-up on, and was dressed in black, and had eaten a pound of Sen-Sen to kill the gin on her breath, and seemed such a devout girl that he forgot his suspicions. (*He pauses.*) Yes, all would have been well, but she was a mischievous minx, and had her own ideas of improving on my joke. When she was saying goodbye to Father Fuller, she added innocently: 'Christ, Father, it's nice and quiet out here away from the damned Sixth Avenue El. I wish to hell I could stay here!' (*Dryly.*) But she didn't, and neither did I.

HOGAN (*chuckles delightedly*). I'll bet you didn't! God bless Dutch Maisie! I'd like to have known her.

TYRONE (*sits down on the steps – with a change of manner*). Well, how's the Duke of Donegal this fine day?

HOGAN. Never better.

TYRONE. Slaving and toiling as usual, I see.

HOGAN. Hasn't a poor man a right to his noon rest without being sneered at by his rich landlord?

TYRONE. 'Rich' is good. I would be, if you'd pay up your back rent.

HOGAN. You ought to pay me, instead, for occupying this rockpile, miscalled a farm. (*His eyes twinkling.*) But I have fine reports to give you of a promising harvest. The milkweed and the thistles is in thriving condition, and I never saw the poison ivy so bounteous and beautiful.

TYRONE *laughs. Without their noticing,* JOSIE *appears in the doorway behind* TYRONE. *She has tidied up and arranged her hair. She smiles down at* JIM, *her face softening, pleased to hear him laugh.*

TYRONE. You win. Where did Josie go, Phil? I saw her here –

HOGAN. She ran in the house to make herself beautiful for you.

JOSIE (*breaks in roughly*). You're a liar. (*To* TYRONE, *her manner one of bold, free-and-easy familiarity.*) Hello, Jim.

TYRONE (*starts to stand up*). Hello, Josie.

JOSIE (*puts a hand on his shoulder and pushes him down*). Don't get up. Sure you know I'm no lady. (*She sits on the top step – banteringly.*) How's my fine Jim this beautiful day? You don't look so bad. You must have stopped at the Inn for an eye-opener – or ten of them.

TYRONE. I've felt worse. (*He looks up at her sardonically.*) And how's my virgin Queen of Ireland?

JOSIE. Yours, is it? Since when? And don't be miscalling me a virgin. You'll ruin my reputation, if you spread that lie about me. (*She laughs. TYRONE is staring at her. She goes on quickly.*) How is it you're around so early? I thought you never got up till afternoon.

TYRONE. Couldn't sleep. One of those heebie-jeebie nights when the booze keeps you awake instead of – (*He catches her giving him a pitying look – irritably.*) But what of it!

JOSIE. Maybe you had no woman in bed with you, for a change. It's a terrible thing to break the habit of years.

TYRONE (*shrugs his shoulders*). Maybe.

JOSIE. What's the matter with the tarts in town, they let you do it? I'll bet the ones you know on Broadway, New York, wouldn't neglect their business.

TYRONE (*pretends to yawn boredly*). Maybe not. (*Then irritably.*) Cut out the kidding, Josie. It's too early.

HOGAN (*who has been taking everything in without seeming to*). I told you not to annoy the gentleman with your rough tongue.

JOSIE. Sure I thought I was doing my duty as hostess making him feel at home.

TYRONE (*stares at her again*). Why all the interest lately in the ladies of the profession, Josie?

JOSIE. Oh, I've been considering joining their union. It's easier living than farming, I'm sure. (*Then resentfully.*) You think I'd starve at it, don't you, because your fancy is for dainty dolls of women? But other men like –

TYRONE (*with sudden revulsion*). For God's sake, cut out that kind of talk, Josie! It sounds like hell.

JOSIE (*stares at him startledly – then resentfully*). Oh, it does, does it? (*Forcing a scornful smile.*) I'm shocking you, I suppose?

HOGAN *is watching them both, not missing anything in their faces, while he seems intent on his pipe.*

TYRONE (*looking a bit sheepish and annoyed at himself for his interest – shrugs his shoulders*). No. Hardly. Forget it. (*He smiles kiddingly.*) Anyway, who told you I fall for the dainty dolls? That's all a thing of the past. I like them tall and strong and voluptuous, now, with beautiful big breasts.

She blushes and looks confused and is furious with herself for doing so.

HOGAN. There you are, Josie, darlin'. Sure he couldn't speak fairer than that.

JOSIE (*recovers herself*). He couldn't, indeed. (*She pats* TYRONE's *head – playfully.*) You're a terrible blarneying liar, Jim, but thank you just the same.

TYRONE *turns his attention to* HOGAN. *He winks at* JOSIE *and begins in an exaggeratedly casual manner.*

TYRONE. I don't blame you, Mr Hogan, for taking it easy on such a blazing hot day.

HOGAN (*doesn't look at him. His eyes twinkle*). Hot, did you say? I find it cool, meself. Take off your coat if you're hot, Mister Tyrone.

TYRONE. One of the most stifling days I've ever known. Isn't it, Josie?

JOSIE (*smiling*). Terrible. I know you must be perishing.

HOGAN. I wouldn't call it a damned bit stifling.

TYRONE. It parches the membranes in your throat.

HOGAN. The what? Never mind. I can't have them, for my throat isn't parched at all. If yours is, Mister Tyrone, there's a well full of water at the back.

TYRONE. Water? That's something people wash with, isn't it? I mean, some people.

HOGAN. So I've heard. But, like you, I find it hard to believe. It's a dirty habit. They must be foreigners.

TYRONE. As I was saying, my throat is parched after the long dusty walk I took just for the pleasure of being your guest.

HOGAN. I don't remember inviting you, and the road is hard macadam with divil a speck of dust, and it's less than a quarter mile from the Inn here.

TYRONE. I didn't have a drink at the Inn. I was waiting until I arrived here, knowing that you –

HOGAN. Knowing I'd what?

TYRONE. Your reputation as a generous host –

HOGAN. The world must be full of liars. So you didn't have a drink at the Inn? Then it must be the air itself smells of whiskey today, although I didn't notice it before you came. You've gone on the water-wagon, I suppose? Well, that's fine, and I ask pardon for misjudging you.

TYRONE. I've wanted to go on the wagon for the past twenty-five years, but the doctors have strictly forbidden it. It would be fatal – with my weak heart.

HOGAN. So you've a weak heart? Well, well, and me thinking it was your head. I'm glad you told me. I was just going to offer you a drink, but whiskey is the worst thing –

TYRONE. The docs say it's a matter of life and death. I must have a stimulant – one big drink at least, whenever I strain my heart walking in the hot sun.

HOGAN. Walk back to the Inn, then, and give it a good strain, so you can buy yourself two big drinks.

JOSIE (*laughing*). Ain't you the fools, playing that old game between you, and both of you pleased as punch!

TYRONE (*gives up with a laugh*). Hasn't he ever been known to loosen up, Josie?

JOSIE. You ought to know. If you need a drink you'll have to buy it from him or die of thirst.

TYRONE. Well, I'll bet this is one time he's going to treat.

HOGAN. Be God, I'll take that bet!

TYRONE. After you've heard the news I've got for you, you'll be so delighted you won't be able to drag out the old bottle quick enough.

HOGAN. I'll have to be insanely delighted.

JOSIE (*full of curiosity*). Shut up, Father. What news, Jim?

TYRONE. I have it off the grapevine that a certain exalted personage will drop in on you before long.

HOGAN. It's the sheriff again. I know by the pleased look on your mug.

TYRONE. Not this time. (*He pauses tantalisingly.*)

JOSIE. Bad luck to you, can't you tell us who?

TYRONE. A more eminent grafter than the sheriff – (*Sneeringly.*) A leading aristocrat in our Land of the Free and Get-Rich-

Quick, whose boots are licked by one and all – one of the Kings of our Republic by Divine Right of Inherited Swag. In short, I refer to your good neighbour, T. Stedman Harder, Standard Oil's sappiest child, whom I know you both love so dearly.

There is a pause after this announcement. HOGAN and JOSIE stiffen, and their eyes begin to glitter. But they can't believe their luck at first.

HOGAN (*in an ominous whisper*). Did you say Harder is coming to call on us, Jim?

JOSIE. It's too good to be true.

TYRONE (*watching them with amusement*). No kidding. The great Mr Harder intends to stop here on his way back to lunch from a horseback ride.

JOSIE. How do you know?

TYRONE. Simpson told me. I ran into him at the Inn.

HOGAN. That English scum of a superintendent!

TYRONE. He was laughing himself sick. He said he suggested the idea to Harder – told him you'd be overwhelmed with awe if he deigned to interview you in person.

HOGAN. Overwhelmed isn't the word. Is it, Josie?

JOSIE. It isn't indeed, Father.

TYRONE. For once in his life, Simpson is cheering for you. He doesn't like his boss. In fact, he asked me to tell you he hopes you kill him.

HOGAN (*disdainfully*). To hell with the Limey's good wishes. I'd like both of them to call together.

JOSIE. Ah, well, we can't have everything. (*To* TYRONE.) What's the reason Mr Harder decided to notice poor, humble scum the like of us?

TYRONE (*grinning*). That's right, Josie. Be humble. He'll expect you to know your place.

HOGAN. Will he now? Well, well. (*With a great happy sigh.*) This is going to be a beautiful day entirely.

JOSIE. But what's Harder's reason, Jim?

TYRONE. Well, it seems he has an ice pond on his estate.

HOGAN. Oho! So that's it!

TYRONE. Yes. That's it. Harder likes to keep up the good old manorial customs. He clings to his ice pond. And your pigpen isn't far from his ice pond.

HOGAN. A nice little stroll for the pigs, that's all.

TYRONE. And somehow Harder's fence in that vicinity has a habit of breaking down.

HOGAN. Fences are queer things. You can't depend on them.

TYRONE. Simpson says he's had it repaired a dozen times, but each time on the following night it gets broken down again.

JOSIE. What a strange thing! It must be the bad fairies. I can't imagine who else could have done it. Can you, Father?

HOGAN. I can't, surely.

TYRONE. Well, Simpson can. He knows you did it and he told his master so.

HOGAN (*disdainfully*). Master is the word. Sure, the English can't live unless they have a lord's backside to kiss, the dirty slaves.

TYRONE. The result of those breaks in the fence is that your pigs stroll – as you so gracefully put it – stroll through to wallow happily along the shores of the ice pond.

HOGAN. Well, why not? Sure, they're fine ambitious American-born pigs and they don't miss any opportunities. They're like Harder's father who made the money for him.

TYRONE. I agree, but for some strange reason Harder doesn't look forward to the taste of pig in next summer's ice water.

HOGAN. He must be delicate. Remember he's delicate, Josie, and leave your club in the house. (*He bursts into joyful menacing laughter.*) Oh, be God and be Christ in the mountains! I've pined to have a quiet word with Mr Harder for years, watching him ride past in his big shiny automobile with his snoot in the air, and being tormented always by the complaints of his Limey superintendent. Oh, won't I welcome him!

JOSIE. Won't *we*, you mean. Sure, I love him as much as you.

HOGAN. I'd kiss you, Jim, for this beautiful news, if you wasn't so damned ugly. Maybe Josie'll do it for me. She has a stronger stomach.

JOSIE. I will! He's earned it. (*She pulls TYRONE's head back and laughingly kisses him on the lips. Her expression changes. She looks startled and confused, stirred and at the same time frightened. She forces a scornful laugh.*) Och, there's no spirit in you! It's like kissing a corpse.

TYRONE (*gives her a strange surprised look – mockingly*). Yes? (*Turning to* HOGAN.) Well, how about that drink, Phil? I'll leave it to Josie if drinks aren't on the house.

HOGAN. *I* won't leave it to Josie. She's prejudiced, being in love.

JOSIE (*angrily*). Shut up, you old liar! (*Then guiltily, forcing a laugh.*) Don't talk nonsense to sneak out of treating Jim.

HOGAN (*sighing*). All right, Josie. Go get the bottle and one small glass, or he'll never stop nagging me. I can turn my back, so the sight of him drinking free won't break my heart.

JOSIE *gets up, laughing, and goes in the house.* HOGAN *peers at the road off left.*

On his way back to lunch, you said? Then it's time – (*Fervently.*) O Holy Joseph, don't let the bastard change his mind.

TYRONE (*beginning to have qualms*). Listen, Phil. Don't get too enthusiastic. He has a big draw around here, and he'll have you pinched, sure as hell, if you beat him up.

HOGAN. Och, I'm no fool.

JOSIE *comes out with a bottle and a tumbler.*

Will you listen to this, Josie. He's warning me not to give Harder a beating – as if I'd dirty my hands on the scum.

JOSIE. As if we'd need to. Sure, all we want is a quiet chat with him.

HOGAN. That's all. As neighbour to neighbour.

JOSIE (*hands* TYRONE *the bottle and tumbler*). Here you are, Jim. Don't stint yourself.

HOGAN (*mournfully*). A fine daughter! I tell you a small glass and you give him a bucket! (*As* TYRONE *pours a big drink, grinning at him, he turns away with a comic shudder.*) That's a fifty-dollar drink, at least.

TYRONE. Here's luck, Phil.

HOGAN. I hope you drown.

TYRONE *drinks and makes a wry face.*

TYRONE. The best chicken medicine I've ever tasted.

HOGAN. That's gratitude for you! Here, pass me the bottle. A drink will warm up my welcome for His Majesty. (*He takes an enormous swig from the bottle.*)

JOSIE (*looking off left*). There's two horseback riders on the county road now.

HOGAN. Praise be to God! It's him and a groom. (*he sets the bottle on top of the boulder.*)

JOSIE. That's McCabe. An old sweetheart of mine. (*She glances at* TYRONE *provokingly – then suddenly worried and protective.*) You get in the house, Jim. If Harder sees you here, he'll lay the whole blame on you.

TYRONE. Nix, Josie. You don't think I'm going to miss this, do you?

JOSIE. You can sit inside by my window and take in everything. Come on, now, don't be stubborn with me. (*She puts her hands under his arms and lifts him to his feet as easily as if he was a child – banteringly.*) Go into my beautiful bedroom. It's a nice place for you.

TYRONE (*kiddingly*). Just what I've been thinking for some time, Josie.

JOSIE (*boldly*). Sure, you've never given me a sign of it. Come up tonight and we'll spoon in the moonlight and you can tell me your thoughts.

TYRONE. That's a date. Remember, now.

JOSIE. It's you who'll forget. Get inside now, before it's too late. (*She gives him a shove inside and closes the door.*)

HOGAN (*has been watching the visitor approach*). He's dismounting – as graceful as a scarecrow, and his poor horse longing to give him a kick. Look at Mac grinning at us. Sit down, Josie. (*She sits on the steps, he on the boulder.*) Pretend you don't notice him.

T. STEDMAN HARDER *appears at left. They act as if they didn't see him.* HOGAN *knocks out his pipe on the palm of his hand.*

HARDER *is in his late thirties but looks younger because his face is unmarked by worry, ambition, or any of the common hazards of life. No matter how long he lives, his four undergraduate years will always be for him the most significant in his life, and the moment of his highest achievement the time he was tapped for an exclusive Senior Society at the Ivy university to which his father had given millions. Since that day he has felt no need for further aspiring, no urge to do anything except settle down on his estate and live the life of a country gentleman, mildly interested in saddle horses and sport models of foreign automobiles. He is not the blatantly silly, playboy heir to millions whose antics make newspaper headlines. He doesn't drink much except when he attends his class reunion every spring – the most exciting episode of each year for him. He doesn't give wild parties, doesn't chase after musical-comedy cuties, is a mildly contented husband and father of three children. A not unpleasant man, affable, good-looking in an ordinary way, sunburnt and healthy, beginning to take on fat, he is simply immature, naturally lethargic, a bit stupid. Coddled from birth, everything arranged and made easy for him, deferred to because of his wealth, he usually has the self-confident attitude of acknowledged superiority, but assumes a supercilious, insecure air when dealing with people beyond his ken. He is dressed in a beautifully tailored English tweed coat and whipcord riding breeches, immaculately polished English riding boots with spurs, and carries a riding crop in his hand.*

It would be hard to find anyone more ill-equipped for combat with the HOGANS. He has never come in contact with anyone like them. To make matters easier for them he is deliberate in his speech, slow on the uptake, and has no sense of humour. The experienced strategy of the Hogans in verbal battle is to take the offensive at once and never let an opponent get set to hit back. Also, they use a beautifully co-ordinated, bewildering change of pace, switching suddenly from jarring shouts to low, confidential vituperation. And they exaggerate their Irish brogues to confuse an enemy still further.

HARDER (*walks toward* HOGAN – *stiffly*). Good morning. I want to see the man who runs this farm.

HOGAN (*surveys him deliberately, his little pig eyes gleaming with malice*). You do, do you? Well, you've seen him. So now run along and play with your horse, and don't bother me. (*He turns to* JOSIE, *who is staring at* HARDER, *much to his discomfiture, as if she had discovered a cockroach in her soup.*) D'you see what I see, Josie? Be God, you'll have to give that damned cat of yours a spanking for bringing it to our doorstep.

HARDER (*determined to be authoritative and command respect – curtly*). Are you Hogan?

HOGAN (*insultingly*). I am *Mister* Philip Hogan – to a gentleman.

JOSIE (*glares at* HARDER). Where's your manners, you spindle-shanked jockey? Were you brought up in a stable?

HARDER (*does not fight with ladies, and especially not with this lady –*

ignoring her). My name is Harder. (*He obviously expects them to be immediately impressed and apologetic.*)

HOGAN (*contemptuously*). Who asked you your name, me little man?

JOSIE. Sure, who in the world cares who the hell you are?

HOGAN. But if you want to play politeness, we'll play with you. Let me introduce you to my daughter, Harder – Miss Josephine Hogan.

JOSIE (*petulantly*). I don't want to meet him, Father. I don't like his silly sheep's face, and I've no use for jockeys, anyway. I'll wager he's no damned good to a woman.

From inside her bedroom comes a burst of laughter. This revelation of an unseen audience startles HARDER. He begins to look extremely unsure of himself.

HOGAN. I don't think he's a jockey. It's only the funny pants he's wearing. I'll bet if you asked his horse, you'd find he's no cowboy either. (*To HARDER, jeeringly.*) Come, tell us the truth, me honey. Don't you kiss your horse each time you mount and beg him, please don't throw me today, darlin', and I'll give you an extra bucket of oats. (*He bursts into an extravagant roar of laughter, slapping his thigh, and JOSIE guffaws with him, while they watch the disconcerting effect of this theatrical mirth on HARDER.*)

HARDER (*beginning to lose his temper*). Listen to me, Hogan! I didn't come here – (*He is going to add 'to listen to your damned jokes' or something like that, but HOGAN silences him.*)

HOGAN (*shouts*). What! What's that you said? (*He stares at the dumbfounded HARDER with droll amazement, as if he couldn't believe his ears.*) You didn't come here? (*He turns to JOSIE in a whisper.*) Did you hear that, Josie? (*He takes off his hat and scratches his head in comic bewilderment.*) Well, that's a puzzle, surely. How d'you suppose he got here?

JOSIE. Maybe the stork brought him, bad luck to it for a dirty bird.

Again TYRONE's laughter is heard from the bedroom.

HARDER (*so off balance now he can only repeat angrily*). I said I didn't come here –

HOGAN (*shouts*). Wait! Wait, now! (*Threateningly.*) We've had enough of that. Say it a third time and I'll send my daughter to telephone the asylum.

HARDER (*forgetting he's a gentleman*). Damn you, I'm the one who's had enough –!

JOSIE (*shouts*). Hold your dirty tongue! I'll have no foul language in my presence.

HOGAN. Och, don't mind him, Josie. He's said he isn't here, anyway, so we won't talk to him behind his back. (*He regards HARDER with pitying contempt.*) Sure, ain't you the poor crazy creature? Do you want us to believe you're your own ghost?

HARDER (*notices the bottle on the boulder for the first time – tries to be contemptuously tolerant and even to smile with condescending disdain*). Ah! I understand now. You're drunk. I'll come back sometime when you're sober – or send Simpson – (*He turns away, glad of an excuse to escape.*)

JOSIE (*jumps up and advances on him menacingly*). No, you don't! You'll apologise first for insulting a lady – insinuating I'm drunk this early in the day – or I'll knock some good breeding in you!

HARDER (*actually frightened now*). I – I said nothing about you –

HOGAN (*gets up to come between them*). Aisy now, Josie. He didn't mean it. He don't know what he means, the poor loon. (*To HARDER – pityingly.*) Run home, that's a good lad, before your keeper misses you.

HARDER (*hastily*). Good day.

He turns eagerly toward left but suddenly HOGAN grabs his shoulder and spins him around – then shifts his grip to the lapel of HARDER's coat.

HOGAN (*grimly*). Wait now, me Honey Boy. I'll have a word with you, if you plaze. I'm beginning to read some sense into this. You mentioned that English bastard, Simpson. I know who you are now.

HARDER (*outraged*). Take your hands off me, you drunken fool. (*He raises his riding crop.*)

JOSIE (*grabs it and tears it from his hand with one powerful twist – fiercely*). Would you strike my poor infirm old father, you coward, you!

HARDER (*calling for help*). McCabe!

HOGAN. Don't think McCabe will hear you, if you blew Gabriel's horn. He knows I or Josie can lick him with one hand. (*Sharply.*) Josie! Stand between us and the gate.

JOSIE *takes her stand where the path meets the road. She turns her back for a moment, shaking with suppressed laughter, and waves her hand at* McCABE *and turns back.* HOGAN *releases his hold on* HARDER's *coat.*

There now. Don't try running away or my daughter will knock you senseless. (*He goes on grimly before* HARDER *can speak.*) You're the blackguard of a millionaire that owns the estate next to ours, ain't you? I've been meaning to call on you, for I've a bone to pick with you, you bloody tyrant! But I couldn't bring myself to set foot on land bought with Standard Oil money that was stolen from the poor it ground in the dust beneath its dirty heel – land that's watered with the tears of starving widows and orphans – (*He abruptly switches from this eloquence to a matter-of-fact tone.*) But never mind that, now. I won't waste words trying to reform a born crook. (*Fiercely, shoving his dirty unshaven face almost into* HARDER's.) What I want to know is, what the hell d'you mean by your contemptible trick of breaking down your fence to entice my poor pigs to take their death in your ice pond?

There is a shout of laughter from JOSIE's *bedroom, and* JOSIE *doubles up and holds her sides.* HARDER *is so flabbergasted by this mad accusation he cannot even sputter. But* HOGAN *acts as if he'd denied it – savagely.*

Don't lie, now! None of your damned Standard Oil excuses, or be Jaysus, I'll break you in half! Haven't I mended that fence morning after morning, and seen the footprints where you had sneaked up in the night to pull it down again. How many times have I mended that fence, Josie?

JOSIE. If it's once, it's a hundred, Father.

HOGAN. Listen, me little millionaire! I'm a peaceful, mild man that believes in live and let live, and as long as the nieghbouring scum leave me alone, I'll let them alone, but when it comes to standing by and seeing my poor pigs murthered one by one –! Josie! How many pigs is it caught their death of cold in his damned ice pond and died of pneumonia?

JOSIE. Ten of them, Father. And ten more died of cholera after drinking the dirty water in it.

HOGAN. All prize pigs, too! I was offered two hundred dollars apiece for them. Twenty pigs at two hundred, that's four thousand. And a thousand to cure the sick and cover funeral expenses for the dead. Call it four thousand you owe me. (*Furiously.*) And you'll pay it, or I'll sue you, so help me Christ! I'll drag you in every court in the land! I'll paste your ugly mug on the front page of every newspaper as a pig-murdering tyrant! Before I'm through with you, you'll think you're the King of England at an Irish wake! (*With a quick change of pace to a wheedling confidential tone.*) Tell me now, if it isn't a secret, whatever made you take such a savage grudge against pigs? Sure, it isn't reasonable for a Standard Oil man to hate hogs.

HARDER (*manages to get in three sputtering words*). I've had enough –!

HOGAN (*with a grin*). Be God, I believe you! (*Switching to fierceness and grabbing his lapel again.*) Look out, now! Keep your place and be soft-spoken to your betters! You're not in your shiny automobile now with your funny nose cocked so you won't smell the poor people. (*He gives him a shake.*) And let me warn you! I have to put up with a lot of pests on this heap of boulders some joker once called a farm. There's a cruel skinflint of a landlord who swindles me out of my last drop of whiskey, and there's poison ivy, and ticks and potato bugs, and there's snakes and skunks! But, be God, I draw the line somewhere, and I'll be damned if I'll stand for a Standard Oil man trespassing! So will you kindly get the hell out of here before I plant a kick on your backside that'll land you in the Atlantic Ocean! (*He gives* HARDER *a shove.*) Beat it now!

HARDER *tries to make some sort of disdainfully dignified exit. But he has to get by* JOSIE.

JOSIE (*leers at him idiotically*). Sure, you wouldn't go without a word of goodbye to me, would you, darlin'? Don't scorn me just because you have on your jockey's pants. (*In a hoarse whisper.*) Meet me tonight, as usual, down by the pigpen.

HARDER'*s retreat becomes a rout. He disappears on left, but a second later his voice, trembling with anger, is heard calling back threateningly.*

HARDER. If you dare touch that fence again, I'll put this matter in the hands of the police!

HOGAN (*shouts derisively*). And I'll put it in my lawyer's hands and in the newspapers! (*He doubles up with glee.*) Look at him fling himself on his nag and spur the poor beast! And look at McCabe behind him! He can hardly stay in the saddle for laughing! (*He slaps his thigh.*) O Jaysus, this is a great day for the poor and oppressed! I'll do no more work! I'll go down to the Inn and spend money and get as drunk as Moses!

JOSIE. Small blame to you. You deserve it. But you'll have your dinner first, to give you a foundation. Come on, now.

They turn back toward the house. From inside another burst of laughter from TYRONE *is heard.* JOSIE *smiles.*

Listen to Jim still in stitches. It's good to hear him laugh as if he meant it.

TYRONE *appears in the doorway of her bedroom.*

TYRONE. O God, my sides are sore.

They all laugh together. He joins them at the left corner of the house.

JOSIE. It's dinner time. Will you have a bite to eat with us, Jim? I'll boil you some eggs.

HOGAN. Och, why do you have to mention eggs? Don't you know it's the one thing he might eat? Well, no matter. Anything goes today. (*He gets the bottle of whiskey.*) Come in, Jim. We'll have a drink while Josie's fixing the grub.

They start to go in the front door, HOGAN *in the lead.*

TYRONE (*suddenly – with sardonic amusement*). Wait a minute. Let us pause to take a look at this very valuable property. Don't you notice the change, Phil? Every boulder on the place has turned to solid gold.

HOGAN. What the hell –? You didn't get the D.T.s from my whiskey, I know that.

TYRONE. No D.T.s about it. This farm has suddenly become a goldmine. You know that offer I told you about? Well, the agent did a little detective work and he discovered it came from Harder. He doesn't want the damned place but he dislikes you as a neighbour and he thinks the best way to get rid of you would be to become your landlord.

HOGAN. The sneaking skunk! I'm sorry I didn't give him that kick.

TYRONE. Yes. So am I. That would have made the place even more valuable. But as it is, you did nobly. I expect him to double or triple his first offer. In fact, I'll bet the sky is the limit now.

HOGAN (*gives* JOSIE *a meaningful look*). I see your point! But we're not worrying you'd ever forget your promise to us for any price.

TYRONE. Promise? What promise? You know what Kipling wrote. (*Paraphrasing the 'Rhyme of the Three Sealers'.*) There's never a promise of God or man goes north of ten thousand bucks.

HOGAN. D'you hear him, Josie? We can't trust him.

JOSIE. Och, you know he's kidding.

HOGAN. I don't. I'm becoming suspicious.

TYRONE (*a trace of bitterness beneath his amused tone*). That's wise dope, Phil. Trust and be a sucker. If I were you, I'd be seriously worried. I've always wanted to own a goldmine – so I could sell it.

JOSIE (*bursts out*). Will you shut up your rotten Broadway blather!

TYRONE (*stares at her in surprise*). Why so serious and indignant, Josie? You just told your unworthy Old Man I was kidding. (*To* HOGAN.) At last, I've got you by the ears, Phil. We must have a serious chat about when you're going to pay that back rent.

HOGAN (*groans*). A landlord who's a blackmailer! Holy God, what next!

JOSIE *is smiling with relief now.*

TYRONE. And you, Josie, please remember when I keep that moonlight date tonight I expect you to be very sweet to me.

JOSIE (*with a bold air*). Sure, you don't have to blackmail me. I'd be that to you, anyway.

HOGAN. Are you laying plots in my presence to seduce my only daughter? (*Then philosophically.*) Well, what can I do? I'll be drunk at the Inn, so how could I prevent it? (*He goes up the steps.*) Let's eat, for the love of God. I'm starving. (*He disappears inside the house.*)

JOSIE (*with an awkward playful gesture, takes* TYRONE *by the hand*). Come along, Jim

TYRONE (*smiles kiddingly*). Afraid you'll lose me? Swell chance!

(*His eyes fix on her breasts – with genuine feeling.*) You have the most beautiful breasts in the world, do you know it, Josie?

JOSIE (*pleased – shyly*). I don't – but I'm happy if you think – (*Then quickly.*) But I've no time now to listen to your kidding, with my mad old father waiting for his dinner. So come on. (*She tugs at his hand and he follows her up the steps. Her manner changes to worried solicitude.*) Promise me you'll eat something, Jim. You've got to eat. You can't go on the way you are, drinking and never eating, hardly. You're killing yourself.

TYRONE (*sardonically*). That's right. Mother me, Josie, I love it.

JOSIE (*bullyingly*). I will, then. You need one to take care of you.

They disappear inside the house.

Curtain.

ACT TWO

Scene. The same, with the wall of the living room removed. It is a clear warm moonlight night, around eleven o'clock. JOSIE is sitting on the steps before the front door. She has changed to her Sunday best, a cheap dark blue dress, black stockings and shoes. Her hair is carefully arranged, and by way of adornment a white flower is pinned on her bosom. She is hunched up, elbows on knees, her chin in her hands. There is an expression on her face we have not seen before, a look of sadness and loneliness and humiliation.

She sighs and gets slowly to her feet, her body stiff from sitting long in the same position. She goes into the living room, fumbles around for a box of matches, and lights a kerosene lamp on the table.

The living room is small, low-ceilinged, with faded, fly-specked wallpaper, a floor of bare boards. It is cluttered up with furniture that looks as if it had been picked up at a fire sale. There is a table at centre, a disreputable old Morris chair beside it; two ugly sideboards, one at left, the other at right-rear; a porch rocking-chair, painted green, with a hole in its cane bottom; a bureau against the rear wall, with two chairs on either side of a door to the kitchen. On the bureau is an alarm clock which shows the time to be five past eleven. At right-front is the door to JOSIE's bedroom.

JOSIE (*looks at the clock – dully*). Five past eleven, and he said he'd be here around nine. (*Suddenly in a burst of humiliated anger, she tears off the flower pinned to her bosom and throws it in the corner.*) To hell with you, Jim Tyrone!

From down the road, the quiet of the night is shattered by a burst of melancholy song. It is unmistakably HOGAN's voice wailing an old Irish lament at the top of his lungs. JOSIE starts – then frowns irritably.

What's bringing him home an hour before the Inn closes? He must be more paralysed than ever I've known him. (*She listens to the singing – grimly.*) Ah, here you come, do you, as full as a tick! I'll give you a welcome, if you start cutting up! I'm in no mood to put up with you.

She goes into her bedroom and returns with her broomstick club.

Outside the singing grows louder as HOGAN *approaches the house.*
He only remembers one verse of the song and he has been repeating it.

HOGAN. Oh, the praties they grow small
Over here, over here,
Oh, the praties they grow small
Over here.
Oh, the praties they grow small
And we dig them in the fall
And we eat them skins and all
Over here, over here.

He enters left-front, weaving and lurching a bit. But he is not as
drunk as he appears. Or rather, he is one of those people who can drink
an enormous amount and be absolutely plastered when they want to be
for their own pleasure, but at the same time are able to pull themselves
together when they wish and be cunningly clear-headed. Just now, he is
letting himself go and getting great satisfaction from it. He pauses and
bellows belligerently at the house.

Hurroo! Down with all tyrants, male and female. To hell with
England, and God damn Standard Oil!

JOSIE (*shouts back*). Shut up your noise, you crazy old billy goat!

HOGAN (*hurt and mournful*). A sweet daughter and a sweet
welcome home in the dead of night. (*Beginning to boil.*) Old
goat! There's respect for you! (*Angrily – starting for the front
door.*) Crazy billy goat, is it? Be God, I'll learn you manners! (*He
pounds on the door with his fist.*) Open the door! Open this door,
I'm saying, before I drive a fist through it, or kick it into
flinders! (*He gives it a kick.*)

JOSIE. It's not locked, you drunken old loon! Open it yourself!

HOGAN (*turns the knob and stamps in*). Drunken old loon, am I? Is
that the way to address your father?

JOSIE. No. It's too damned good for him.

HOGAN. It's time I taught you a lesson. Be Jaysus, I'll take you
over my knee and spank your tail, if you are as big as a cow!
(*He makes a lunge to grab her.*)

JOSIE. Would you, though! Take that, then! (*She raps him smartly,
but lightly, on his bald spot with the end of her broom handle.*)

HOGAN (*with an exaggerated howl of pain*). Ow! (*His anger
evaporates and he rubs the top of his head ruefully – with bitter*

complaint.) God forgive you, it's a great shame to me I've raised a daughter so cowardly she has to use a club.

JOSIE (*puts her club on the table – grimly*). Now I've no club.

HOGAN (*evades the challenge*). I never thought I'd see the day when a daughter of mine would be such a coward as to threaten her old father when he's helpless drunk and can't hit back. (*He slumps down on the Morris chair.*)

JOSIE. Ah, that's better. Now that little game is over. (*Then angrily.*) Listen to me, Father. I have no patience left, so get up from that chair, and go in your room, and go to bed, or I'll take you by the scruff of your neck and the seat of your pants and throw you in and lock the door on you! I mean it, now! (*On the verge of angry tears.*) I've had all I can bear this night, and I want some peace and sleep, and not to listen to an old lush!

HOGAN (*appears drunker, his head wagging, his voice thick, his talk rambling*). That's right. Fight with me. My own daughter has no feelings or sympathy. As if I hadn't enough after what's happened tonight.

JOSIE (*with angry disgust*). Och, don't try – (*Then curiously.*) What's happened? I thought something must be queer, you coming home before the Inn closed, but then I thought maybe for once you'd drunk all you could hold. (*Scathingly.*) And, God pity you, if you ain't that full, you're damned close to it.

HOGAN. Go on. Make fun of me. Old lush! You wouldn't feel so comical, if – (*He stops, mumbling to himself.*)

JOSIE. If what?

HOGAN. Never mind. Never mind. I didn't come home to fight, but seek comfort in your company. And if I was singing coming along the road, it was only because there's times you have to sing to keep from crying.

JOSIE. I can see you crying!

HOGAN. You will. And you'll see yourself crying, too, when – (*He stops again and mumbles to himself.*)

JOSIE. When what? (*Exasperatedly.*) Will you stop your whiskey drooling and talk plain?

HOGAN (*thickly*). No matter. No matter. Leave me alone.

JOSIE (*angrily*). That's good advice. To hell with you! I know your game. Nothing at all has happened. All you want is to keep me up listening to your guff. Go to your room, I'm saying, before –

HOGAN. I won't. I couldn't sleep with my thoughts tormented the way they are. I'll stay here in this chair, and you go to your room and let me be.

JOSIE (*snorts*). And have you singing again in a minute and smashing the furniture –

HOGAN. Sing, is it? Are you making fun again? I'd give a keen of sorrow or howl at the moon like an old mangy hound in his sadness if I knew how, but I don't. So rest aisy. You won't hear a sound from me. Go on and snore like a pig to your heart's content. (*He mourns drunkenly.*) A fine daughter! I'd get more comfort from strangers.

JOSIE. Och, for God's sake, dry up! You'll sit in the dark then. I won't leave the lamp lit for you to turn over and burn down the house. (*She reaches out to turn down the lamp.*)

HOGAN (*thickly*). Let it burn to the ground. A hell of a lot I care if it burns.

JOSIE (*in the act of turning down the lamp, stops and stares at him, puzzled and uneasy*). I never heard you talk that way before, no matter how drunk you were. (*He mumbles. Her tone becomes persuasive.*) What's happened to you, Father?

HOGAN (*bitterly*). Ah, it's 'Father' now, is it, not old billy goat? Well, thank God for small favours. (*With heavy sarcasm.*) Oh, nothing's happened to me at all, at all. A trifle, only. I wouldn't waste your time mentioning it, or keep you up when you want sleep so bad.

JOSIE (*angrily*). Och, you old loon, I'm sick of you. Sleep it off till you get some sense. (*She reaches for the lamp again.*)

HOGAN. Sleep it off? We'll see if you sleep it off when you know – (*He lapses into drunken mumbling.*)

JOSIE (*again stares at him*). Know what, Father?

HOGAN (*mumbles*). The son of a bitch!

JOSIE (*trying a lighter tone*). Sure, there's a lot of those in the neighbourhood. Which one do you mean? Is Harder on your mind again?

HOGAN (*thickly*). He's one and a prize one, but I don't mean him. I'll say this for Harder, you know what to expect from him. He's no wolf in sheep's clothing, nor a treacherous snake in the grass who stabs you in the back with a knife –

JOSIE (*apprehensive now – forces a joke*). Sure, if you've found a snake who can stab you with a knife, you'd better join the circus with him and make a pile of money.

HOGAN (*bitterly*). Make jokes, God forgive you! You'll soon laugh from the wrong end of your mouth! (*He mumbles.*) Pretending he's our friend! The lying bastard!

JOSIE (*bristles resentfully*). Is it Jim Tyrone you're calling hard names?

HOGAN. That's right. Defend him, you big soft fool! Faith, you're a prize dunce! You've had a good taste of believing his word, waiting hours for him dressed up in your best like a poor sheep without pride or spirit –

JOSIE (*stung*). Shut up! I was calling him a lying bastard myself before you came, and saying I'd never speak to him again. And I knew all along he'd never remember to keep his date after he got drunk.

HOGAN. He's not so drunk he forgot to attend to business.

JOSIE (*as if she hadn't heard – defiantly*). I'd have stayed up anyway a beautiful night like this to enjoy the moonlight, if there wasn't a Jim Tyrone in the world.

HOGAN (*with heavy sarcasm*). In your best shoes and stockings? Well, well. Sure, the moon must feel flattered by your attentions.

JOSIE (*furiously*). You won't feel flattered if I knock you tail over tincup out of that chair! And stop your whiskey gabble about Jim. I see what you're driving at with your dark hints and curses, and if you think I'll believe – (*With forced assurance.*) Sure, I know what's happened as well as if I'd been there. Jim saw you'd got drunker than usual and you were an easy mark for a joke, and he's made a goat of you!

HOGAN (*bitterly*). Goat, again! (*He struggles from his chair and stands swaying unsteadily – with offended dignity.*) All right, I won't say another word. There's no use telling the truth to a bad-tempered woman in love.

JOSIE. Love be damned! I hate him now!

HOGAN. Be Christ, you have me stumped. A great proud slut who's played games with half the men around here, and now you act like a numbskull virgin that can't believe a man would tell her a lie!

JOSIE (*threateningly*). If you're going to your room, you'd better go quick!

HOGAN (*fixes his eyes on the door at rear – with dignity*). That's where I'm going, yes – to talk to meself so I'll know someone with brains is listening. Good night to you, Miss Hogan. (*He starts – swerves left – tries to correct this and lurches right and bumps against her, clutching the supporting arm she stretches out.*)

JOSIE. God help you, if you try to go upstairs now, you'll end up in the cellar.

HOGAN (*hanging on to her arm and shoulder – maudlinly affectionate now*). You're right. Don't listen to me. I'm wrong to bother you. You've had sorrow enough this night. Have a good sleep, while you can, Josie, darlin' – and good night and God bless you. (*He tries to kiss her, but she wards him off and steers him back to the chair.*)

JOSIE. Sit down before you split in pieces on the floor and I have to get the wheelbarrow to collect you. (*She dumps him in the chair where he sprawls limply, his chin on his chest.*)

HOGAN (*mumbles dully*). It's too late. It's all settled. We're helpless, entirely.

JOSIE (*really worried now*). How is it all settled? If you're helpless, I'm not. (*Then as he doesn't reply – scornfully.*) It's the first time I ever heard you admit you were licked. And it's the first time I ever saw you so paralysed you couldn't shake the whiskey from your brains and get your head clear when you wanted. Sure, that's always been your pride – and now look at you, the stupid object you are, mumbling and drooling!

HOGAN (*struggles up in his chair – angrily*). Shut up your insults! Be God, I can get my head clear if I like! (*He shakes his head violently.*) There! It's clear. I can tell you each thing that happened tonight as clear as if I'd not taken a drop, if you'll listen and not keep calling me a liar.

JOSIE. I'll listen, now I see you have hold of your wits.

HOGAN. All right, then. I'll begin at the beginning when him and me left here, and you gave him a sweet smile, and rolled your big beautiful cow's eyes at him, and wiggled your backside, and stuck out your beautiful breasts you know he admires, and said in a sick sheep's voice, 'Don't forget our moonlight date, Jim.'

JOSIE (*with suppressed fury*). You're a –! I never –! You old –!

HOGAN. And he said: 'You bet I won't forget, Josie.'

JOSIE. The lying crook!

HOGAN (*his voice begins to sink into a dejected monotone*). We went to the Inn and started drinking whiskey. And I got drunk.

JOSIE (*exasperatedly*). I guessed that! And Jim got drunk, too. And then what?

HOGAN (*dully*). Who knows how drunk he got? He had one of his queer fits when you can't tell. He's the way I told you about this morning, when he talks like a Broadway crook, who'd sell his soul for a price, and there's a sneering divil in him, and he loves to pick out the weakness in people and say cruel, funny things that flay the hide off them, or play cruel jokes on them. (*With sudden rage.*) God's curse on him, I'll wager he's laughing to himself this minute, thinking it's the cutest joke in the world, the fools he's made of us. You in particular. Be God, I had my suspicions, at least, but your head was stuffed with mush and love, and you wouldn't –

JOSIE (*furiously*). You'll tell that lie about my love once too often! And I'll play a joke on him yet that'll make him sorry he –

HOGAN (*sunk in drunken defeatism again*). It's too late. You shouldn't have let him get away from you to the Inn. You should have kept him here. Then maybe, if you'd got him drunk enough you could have – (*His head nodding, his eyes blinking – thickly.*) But it's no good talking now – no good at all – no good –

JOSIE (*gives him a shake*). Keep hold of your wits or I'll give you a cuff on both ears! Will you stop blathering like an old woman and tell me plainly what he's done!

HOGAN. He's agreed to sell the farm, that's what! Simpson came to the Inn to see him with a new offer from Harder. Ten thousand, cash.

JOSIE (*overwhelmed*). Ten thousand! Sure, three is all it's worth at most. And two was what you offered that Jim promised –

HOGAN. What's money to Harder? After what we did to him, all he wants is revenge. And here's where he's foxy. Simpson must have put him up to it knowing how Jim hates it here living on a small allowance, and he longs to go back to Broadway and his whores. Jim won't have to wait for his half of the cash till the estate's settled. Harder offers to give him five thousand cash as a loan against the estate the second the sale is made. Jim can take the next train to New York.

JOSIE (*tensely, on the verge of tears*). And Jim accepted? I don't believe it!

HOGAN. Don't then. Be God, you'll believe it tomorrow! Harder proposed that he meet with Jim and the executors in the morning and settle it, and Jim promised Simpson he would.

JOSIE (*desperately*). Maybe he'll get so drunk he'll never remember –

HOGAN. He won't. Harder's coming in his automobile to pick him up and make sure of him. Anyway don't think because he forgot you were waiting – in the moonlight, eating your heart out, that he'd ever miss a date with five thousand dollars, and all the pretty whores of Broadway he can buy with it.

JOSIE (*distractedly*). Will you shut up! (*Angrily.*) And where were you when all this happened? Couldn't you do anything to stop it, you old loon?

HOGAN. I couldn't. Simpson came and sat at the table with us –

JOSIE. And you let him!

HOGAN. Jim invited him. Anyway, I wanted to find out what trick he had up his sleeve, and what Jim would do. When it was all over, I got up and took a swipe at Simpson, but I missed him. (*With drunken sadness.*) I was too drunk – too drunk – too drunk – I missed him, God forgive me! (*His chin sinks on his chest and his eyes shut.*)

JOSIE (*shakes him*). If you don't keep awake, be God, I won't miss you!

HOGAN. I was going to take a swipe at Jim, too, but I couldn't do it. My heart was too broken with sorrow, I'd come to love him like a son – a real son of my heart! – to take the place of that jackass, Mike, and me two other jackasses.

JOSIE (*her face hard and bitter*). I think now Mike was the only one in this house with sense.

HOGAN. I was too drowned in sorrow by his betraying me – and you he'd pretended to like so much. So I only called him a dirty lying skunk of a treacherous bastard, and I turned my back on him and left the Inn, and I made myself sing on the road so he'd hear, and they'd all hear in the Inn, to show them I didn't care a damn.

JOSIE (*scathingly*). Sure, wasn't you the hero! A hell of a lot of good —

HOGAN. Ah, well, I suppose the temptation was too great. He's weak, with one foot in the grave from whiskey. Maybe we shouldn't blame him.

ᵀOSIE (*her eyes flashing*). Not blame him? Well, I blame him, God damn him! Are you making excuses for him, you old fool?

HOGAN. I'm not. He's a dirty snake! But I was thinking how do I know what I wouldn't do for five thousand cash, and how do you know what you wouldn't do?

JOSIE. Nothing could make me betray him! (*Her face grows hard and bitter.*) Or it couldn't before. There's nothing I wouldn't do now.

HOGAN *suddenly begins to chuckle.*

Do you think I'm lying? Just give me a chance —

HOGAN. I remembered something. (*He laughs drunkenly.*) Be Christ, Josie, for all his Broadway wisdom about women, you've made a prize damned fool of him and that's some satisfaction!

JOSIE (*bewildered*). How'd you mean?

HOGAN. You'll never believe it. Neither did I, but he kept on until, be God, I saw he really meant it.

JOSIE. Meant what?

HOGAN. It was after he'd turned queer — early in the night before Simpson came. He started talking about you, as if you was on his mind, worrying him — and before he finished I take my oath I began to hope you could really work Mike's first scheme on him, if you got him alone in the moonlight, because all his gab was about his great admiration for you.

JOSIE. Och! The liar!

HOGAN. He said you had great beauty in you that no one appreciated but him.

JOSIE (*shakenly*). You're lying.

HOGAN. Great strength you had, and great pride, he said – and great goodness, no less! But here's where you've made a prize jackass of him, like I said. (*With a drunken leer.*) Listen now, darlin', and don't drop dead with amazement. (*He leans toward her and whispers.*) He believes you're a virgin!

JOSIE *stiffens as if she'd been insulted.* HOGAN *goes on.*

He does, so help me! He means it, the poor dunce! He thinks you're a poor innocent virgin! He thinks it's all boasting and pretending you've done about being a slut. (*He chuckles.*) A virgin, no less! You!

JOSIE (*furiously*). Stop saying it! Boasting and pretending, am I? The dirty liar!

HOGAN. Faith, you don't have to tell me. (*Then he looks at her in drunken surprise – thickly.*) Are you taking it as an insult? Why the hell don't you laugh? Be God, you ought to see what a stupid sheep that makes him.

JOSIE (*forces a laugh*). I do see it.

HOGAN (*chuckling drunkenly*). Oh, be God, I've just remembered another thing, Josie. I know why he didn't keep his date with you. It wasn't that he'd forgot. He remembered well enough, for he talked about it –

JOSIE. You mean he deliberately, knowing I'd be waiting – (*Fiercely.*) God damn him!

HOGAN. He as much as told me his reason, though he wouldn't come out with it plain, me being your father. His conscience was tormenting him. He's going to leave you alone and not see you again – for your sake, because he loves you! (*He chuckles.*)

JOSIE (*looks stricken and bewildered – her voice trembling*). Loves me? You're making it up.

HOGAN. I'm not. I know it sounds crazy but –

JOSIE. What did he mean, for my sake?

HOGAN. Can't you see? You're a pure virgin to him, but all the same there's things besides your beautiful soul he feels drawn to, like your beautiful hair and eyes, and –

JOSIE (*strickenly*). Och, don't, Father! You know I'm only a big –

HOGAN (*as if she hadn't spoken*). So he'll keep away from temptation because he can't trust himself, and it'd be a sin on his conscience if he was to seduce you. (*He laughs drunkenly*.) Oh, be God! If that ain't rich!

JOSIE (*her voice trembles*). So that was his reason – (*Then angrily*.) So he thinks all he has to do is crook a finger and I'll fall for him, does he, the vain Broadway crook!

HOGAN (*chuckling*). Be Jaysus, it was the maddest thing in the world, him gabbing like a soft loon about you – and there at the bar in plain sight was two of the men you've been out with, the gardener at Smith's and Regan, the chauffeur for Driggs, having a drink together!

JOSIE (*with a twitching smile*). It must have been mad, surely. I wish I'd been there to laugh up my sleeve. (*Angry*.) But what's all his crazy lying blather got to do with him betraying us and selling the place?

HOGAN (*at once hopelessly dejected again*). Nothing at all. I only thought you'd like to know you'd had that much revenge.

JOSIE. A hell of a revenge! I'll have a better one than that on him – or I'll try to! I'm not like you, owning up I'm beaten and crying wurra-wurra like a coward and getting hopeless drunk! (*She gives him a shake*.) Get your wits about you and answer me this: Did Simpson get him to sign a paper?

HOGAN. No, but what good is that? In the morning he'll sign all they shove in front of him.

JOSIE. It's this good. It means we still have a chance. Or I have.

HOGAN. What chance? Are you going to beg him to take pity on us?

JOSIE. I'll see him in hell first! There's another chance, and a good one. But I'll need your help – (*Angrily*.) And look at you, your brains drowned in whiskey, so I can't depend on you!

HOGAN (*rousing himself*). You can, if there's any chance. Be God, I'll make myself as sober as a judge for you in the wink of an eye! (*Then dejectedly*.) But what can you do now, darlin'? You haven't even got him here. He's down at the Inn sitting alone, drinking and dreaming of the little whores he'll be with tomorrow night on Broadway.

JOSIE. I'll get him here! I'll humble my pride and go down to the Inn for him! And if he doesn't want to come I've a way to make him. I'll raise a scene and pretend I'm in a rage because he forgot his date. I'll disgrace him till he'll be glad to come with me to shut me up. I know his weakness, and it's his vanity about his women. If I was a dainty, pretty tart he'd be proud I'd raise a rumpus about him. But when it's a big, ugly hulk like me — (*She falters and forces herself to go on.*) If he ever was tempted to want me, he'd be ashamed of it. That's the truth behind the lies he told you of his conscience and his fear he might ruin me, God damn him!

HOGAN. No, he meant it, Josie. But never mind that now. Let's say you've got him here. Then what will you do?

JOSIE. I told you this morning if he ever broke his promise to us I'd do anything and not mind how crooked it was. And I will! Your part in it is to come at sunrise with witnesses and catch us in — (*She falters.*)

HOGAN. In bed, is it? Then it's Mike's second scheme you're thinking about?

JOSIE. I told you I didn't care how dirty a trick — (*With a hard bitter laugh.*) The dirtier the better now!

HOGAN. But how'll you get him in bed, with all his honourable scruples, thinking you're a virgin? But I'm forgetting he stayed away because he was afraid he'd be tempted. So maybe —

JOSIE (*tensely*). For the love of God, don't harp on his lies. He won't be tempted at all. But I'll get him so drunk he'll fall asleep and I'll carry him in and put him in bed —

HOGAN. By God, that's the way! But you'll have to get a pile of whiskey down him. You'll never do it unless you're more sociable and stop looking at him, the way you do, whenever he takes a drink, as if you was praying Almighty God to forgive a poor drunkard. You've got to encourage him. The best way would be for you to drink with him. It would put him at his ease and unsuspecting, and it'd give you courage, too, so you'd act bold for a change instead of giving him brazen talk he's tired of hearing, while you act shy as a mouse.

JOSIE (*gives her father a bitter, resentful look*). You're full of sly advice all of a sudden, ain't you? You dirty little tick!

HOGAN (*angrily*). Didn't you tell me to get hold of my wits? Be God, if you want me drunk, I've only to let go. That'd suit me. I want to forget my sorrow, and I've no faith in your scheme because you'll be too full of scruples. Like the drinking. You're such a virtuous teetotaller —

JOSIE. I've told you I'd do anything now! (*Then confusedly.*) All I meant was, it's not right, a father to tell his daughter how to — (*Then angrily.*) I don't need your advice. Haven't I had every man I want around here?

HOGAN. Ah, thank God, that sounds natural! Be God, I thought you'd started playing virgin with me just because that Broadway sucker thinks you're one.

JOSIE (*furiously*). Shut up! I'm not playing anything. And don't worry I can't do my part of the trick.

HOGAN. That's the talk! But let me get it all clear. I come at sunrise with my witnesses, and you've forgot to lock your door, and we walk in, and there's the two of you in bed, and I raise the roof and threaten him if he don't marry you —

JOSIE. Marry him? After what he's done to us? I wouldn't marry him now if he was the last man on earth! All we want is a paper signed by him with witnesses that he'll sell the farm to you for the price you offered, and not to Harder.

HOGAN. Well, that's justice, but that's all it is. I thought you wanted to make him pay for his black treachery against us, the dirty bastard!

JOSIE. I do want! (*She again gives him a bitter resentful glance.*) It's the estate money you're thinking of, isn't it? Leave it to you! (*Hastily.*) Well, so am I! I'd like to get my hooks on it! (*With a hard, brazen air.*) Be God, if I'm to play whore, I deserve my pay! We'll make him sign a paper he owes me ten thousand dollars the minute the estate is settled. (*She laughs.*) How's that? I'll bet none of his tarts on Broadway ever got a thousandth part of that out of him, no matter how dainty and pretty! (*Laughing again.*) And here's what'll be the greatest joke to teach him a lesson. He'll pay it for nothing! I'll get him in bed but I'll never let him —

HOGAN (*with delighted admiration*). Och, by Jaysus, Josie, that's the best yet! (*He slaps his thigh enthusiastically.*) Oh, that'll teach him to double-cross his friends! That'll show him two can play at tricks! And him believing you so innocent! Be God, you'll make him the prize sucker of the world! Won't I roar inside me when I see his face in the morning! (*He bursts into coarse laughter.*)

JOSIE (*again with illogical resentment*). Stop laughing! You're letting yourself be drunk again. (*Then with a hard, business-like air.*) We've done enough talking. Let's start —

HOGAN. Wait, now. There's another thing. Just what do you want me to threaten him with when I catch you? That we'll sue him for outraging your virtue? Sure, his lawyer would have all your old flames in the witness box, till the jury would think you'd been faithful to the male inhabitants of America. So what threat – I can't think of any he wouldn't laugh at.

JOSIE (*tensely*). Well, I can! Do I have to tell you his weakness again? It's his vanity about women, and his Broadway pride he's so wise no woman could fool him. It's the disgrace to his vanity – being caught with the likes of me – (*Falteringly, but forcing herself to go on.*) My mug beside his in all the newspapers – the New York papers, too – he'll see the whole of Broadway splitting their sides laughing at him – and he'll give anything to keep us quiet, I tell you. He will! I know him! So don't worry – (*She ends up on the verge of bitter humiliated tears.*)

HOGAN (*without looking at her – enthusiastic again*). Be God, you're right!

JOSIE (*gives him a bitter glance – fiercely*). Then get the hell out of that chair and let's start it! (*He gets up. She surveys him resentfully.*) You're steady on your pins, ain't you, you scheming old thief, now there's the smell of money around! (*Quickly.*) Well, I'm glad. I know I can depend on you now. You'll walk down to the Inn with me and hide outside until you see me come out with him. Then you can sneak in the Inn yourself and pick the witnesses to stay up with you. But mind you don't get drunk again, and let them get too drunk.

HOGAN. I won't, I take my oath! (*He pats her on the shoulder approvingly.*) Be God, you've got the proud, fighting spirit in you that never says die, and you make me ashamed of my weakness. You're that eager now, be damned if I don't almost think you're glad of the excuse!

JOSIE (*stiffens*). Excuse for what, you old –

HOGAN. To show him no man can get the best of you – what else? – like you showed all the others.

JOSIE. I'll show him to his sorrow! (*Then abruptly, starting for the screen door at left.*) Come on. We've no time to waste. (*But when she gets to the door, she appears suddenly hesitant and timid – hurriedly.*) Wait. I'd better give a look at myself in the mirror. (*In a brazen tone.*) Sure, those in my trade have to look their best! (*She hurries back across the room into her bedroom and closes the door.*)

HOGAN *stares after her. Abruptly he ceases to look like a drunk who, by an effort, is keeping himself half-sober. He is a man who has been drinking a lot but is still clear-headed and has complete control of himself.*

HOGAN (*watches the crack under* JOSIE's *door and speaks half-aloud to himself, shaking his head pityingly*). A look in the mirror and she's forgot to light her lamp! (*Remorsefully.*) God forgive me, it's bitter medicine. But it's the only way I can see that has a chance now.

JOSIE's *door opens. At once he is as he was. She comes out, a fixed smile on her lips, her head high, her face set defiantly. But she has evidently been crying.*

JOSIE (*brazenly*). There, now. Don't I look ten thousand dollars' worth to any drunk?

HOGAN. You look a million, darlin'!

JOSIE (*goes to the screen door and pushes it open with the manner of one who has burned all bridges*). Come along, then. (*She goes out. He follows close on her heels. She stops abruptly on the first step – startledly.*) Look! There's someone on the road –

HOGAN (*pushes past her down the steps – peering off left-front – as if aloud to himself, in dismay*). Be God, it's him! I never thought –

JOSIE (*as if aloud to herself*). So he didn't forget –

HOGAN (*quickly*). Well, it proves he can't keep away from you, and that'll make it easier for you – (*Then furiously.*) Oh, the dirty, double-crossing bastard! The nerve of him! Coming to call on you, after making you wait for hours, thinking you don't know what he's done to us this night, and it'll be a fine cruel joke to blarney you in the moonlight, and you trusting him like a poor sheep, and never suspecting –

JOSIE (*stung*). Shut up! I'll teach him who's the joker! I'll let him go on as if you hadn't told me what he's done –

HOGAN. Yes, don't let him suspect it, or you wouldn't fool him. He'd know you were after revenge. But he can see me here now. I can't sneak away or he'd be suspicious. We've got to think of a new scheme quick to get me away –

JOSIE (*quickly*). I know how. Pretend you're as drunk as when you came. Make him believe you're so drunk you don't remember what he's done, so he can't suspect you told me.

HOGAN. I will. Be God, Josie, damned if I don't think he's so queer drunk himself he don't remember, or he'd never come here.

JOSIE. The drunker he is the better! (*Lowering her voice – quickly.*) He's turned in the gate where he can hear us. Pretend we're fighting and I'm driving you off till you're sober. Say you won't be back tonight. It'll make him sure he'll have the night alone with me. You start the fight.

HOGAN (*becomes at once very drunk. He shouts*). Put me out of my own home, will you, you undutiful slut!

JOSIE. Celebration or not, I'll have no drunks cursing and singing all night. Go back to the Inn.

HOGAN. I will! I'll get a room and two bottles and stay drunk as long as I please!

JOSIE. Don't come back till you've slept it off, or I'll wipe the floor with you!

TYRONE *enters, left-front. He does not appear to be drunk – that is, he shows none of the usual symptoms. He seems much the same as in Act One. The only perceptible change is that his eyes have a peculiar fixed, glazed look, and there is a certain vague quality in his manner and speech, as if he were a bit hazy and absent-minded.*

TYRONE (*dryly*). Just in time for the Big Bout. Or is this the final round?

HOGAN (*whirls on him unsteadily*). Who the hell – (*Peering at him.*) Oh, it's you, is it?

TYRONE. What was the big idea, Phil, leaving me flat?

HOGAN. Leave you flat? Be Jaysus, that reminds me I owe you a swipe on the jaw for something. What was it? Be God, I'm too drunk to remember. But here it is, anyway.

He turns loose a round-house swing that misses TYRONE by a couple of feet, and reels away. TYRONE regards him with vague surprise.

JOSIE. Stop it, you damned old fool, and get out of here!

HOGAN. Taking his side against your poor old father, are you? A hell of a daughter! (*He draws himself up with drunken dignity.*) Don't expect me home tonight, Miss Hogan, or tomorrow either, maybe. You can take your bad temper out on your sweetheart, here. (*He starts off down the road, left-front, with a last word over his shoulder.*) Bad luck to you both. (*He disappears. A moment later he begins to bawl his mournful Irish song.*) 'Oh, the praties they grow small, Over here, over here,' etc.

During a part of the following scene the song continues to be heard at intervals, receding as he gets farther off on his way to the Inn.

JOSIE. Well, thank God. That's good riddance. (*She comes to* TYRONE, *who stands staring after* HOGAN *with a puzzled look.*)

TYRONE. I've never seen him that stinko before. Must have got him all of a sudden. He didn't seem so lit up at the Inn, but I guess I wasn't paying much attention.

JOSIE (*forcing a playful air*). I should think, if you were a real gentleman, you'd be apologising to me, not thinking of him. Don't you know you're two hours and a half late? I oughtn't to speak to you, if I had any pride.

TYRONE (*stares at her curiously*). You've got too damn much pride, Josie. That's the trouble.

JOSIE. And just what do you mean by that, Jim?

TYRONE (*shrugs his shoulders*). Nothing. Forget it. I do apologise, Josie. I'm damned sorry. Haven't any excuse. Can't think up a lie. (*Staring at her curiously again.*) Or, now I think of it, I had a damned good honourable excuse, but – (*He shrugs.*) Nuts. Forget it.

JOSIE. Holy Joseph, you're full of riddles tonight. Well, I don't need excuses. I forgive you, anyway, now you're here. (*She takes his hand – playfully.*) Come on now, and we'll sit on my bedroom steps and be romantic in the moonlight, like we planned to. (*She leads him there. He goes along in an automatic way, as if only half-conscious of what he is doing. She sits on the top step and pulls him down on the step beneath her. A pause. He stares vaguely at nothing. She bends to give him an uneasy appraising glance.*)

TYRONE (*suddenly, begins to talk mechanically*). Had to get out of the damned Inn. I was going batty alone there. The old heebie-jeebies. So I came to you. (*He pauses – then adds with strange, wondering sincerity.*) I've really begun to love you a lot, Josie.

JOSIE (*blurts out bitterly*). Yes, you've proved that tonight, haven't you? (*Hurriedly regaining her playful tone.*) But never mind. I said I'd forgive you for being so late. So go on about love. I'm all ears.

TYRONE (*as if he hadn't listened*). I thought you'd have given me up and gone to bed. I remember I had some nutty idea I'd get in bed with you – just to lie with my head on your breast.

JOSIE (*moves in spite of herself – but keeps her bold, playful tone*).
Well, maybe I'll let you – (*Hurriedly.*) Later on, I mean. The
night's young yet, and we'll have it all to ourselves. (*Boldly
again.*) But here's for a starter. (*She puts her arms around him and
draws him back till his head is on her breast.*) There, now.

TYRONE (*relaxes – simply and gratefully*). Thanks, Josie. (*He closes
his eyes.*)

*For a moment, she forgets everything and stares down at his face with a
passionate, possessive tenderness. A pause. From far-off on the road to
the Inn, HOGAN's mournful song drifts back through the moonlight
quiet: 'Oh, the praties they grow small, Over here, over here.'
TYRONE rouses himself and straightens up. He acts embarrassed, as
if he felt he'd been making a fool of himself – mockingly.*

Hark, Hark, the Donegal lark! 'Thou wast not born for death,
immortal bird.' Can't Phil sing anything but that damned dirge,
Josie? (*She doesn't reply. He goes on hazily.*) Still, it seems to belong
tonight – in the moonlight – or in my mind – (*He quotes.*)

Now more than ever seems it rich to die,
To cease upon the midnight with no pain,
In such an ecstasy!

(*He has recited this with deep feeling. Now he sneers.*) Good God!
Ode to Phil the Irish Nightingale! I must have the D.T.s.

JOSIE (*her face grown bitter*). Maybe it's only your bad conscience.

TYRONE (*starts guiltily and turns to stare into her face – suspiciously*).
What put that in your head? Conscience about what?

JOSIE (*quickly*). How would I know, if you don't? (*Forcing a
playful tone.*) For the sin of wanting to be in bed with me.
Maybe that's it.

TYRONE (*with strange relief*). Oh. (*A bit shamefacedly.*) Forget that
stuff, Josie. I was half nutty.

JOSIE (*bitterly*). Och, for the love of God, don't apologise as if
you was ashamed of – (*She catches herself.*)

TYRONE (*with a quick glance at her face*). All right. I certainly
won't apologise – if you're not kicking. I was afraid I might
have shocked your modesty.

JOSIE (*roughly*). My modesty? Be God, I didn't know I had any
left.

TYRONE (*draws away from her – irritably*). Nix, Josie. Lay off that line, for tonight at least. (*He adds slowly.*) I'd like tonight to be different.

JOSIE. Different from what? (*He doesn't answer. She forces a light tone.*) All right. I'll be as different as you please.

TYRONE (*simply*). Thanks, Josie. Just be yourself. (*Again as if he were ashamed, or afraid he had revealed some weakness — off-handedly.*) This being out in the moonlight instead of the lousy Inn isn't a bad bet, at that. I don't know why I hang out in that dump, except I'm even more bored in the so-called good hotels in this hick town.

JOSIE (*trying to examine his face without his knowing*). Well, you'll be back on Broadway soon now, won't you?

TYRONE. I hope so.

JOSIE. Then you'll have all the pretty little tarts to comfort you when you get your sorrowful spell on.

TYRONE. Oh, to hell with the rough stuff, Josie! You promised you'd can it tonight.

JOSIE (*tensely*). You're a fine one to talk of promises!

TYRONE (*vaguely surprised by her tone*). What's the matter? Still sore at me for being late?

JOSIE (*quickly*). I'm not. I was teasing you. To prove there's no hard feelings, how would you like a drink? But I needn't ask. (*She gets up.*) I'll get a bottle of his best.

TYRONE (*mechanically*). Fine. Maybe that will have some kick. The booze at the Inn didn't work tonight.

JOSIE. Well, this'll work. (*She starts to go into her bedroom.*)

He sits hunched up on the step, staring at nothing. She pauses in the doorway to glance back. The hard, calculating expression on her face softens. For a second she stares at him, bewildered by her conflicting feelings. Then she goes inside, leaving the door open. She opens the door from her room to the lighted living-room, and is seen going to the kitchen on the way to the cellar. She has left the door from the living room to her bedroom open and the light reveals a section of the bedroom framed in the doorway behind TYRONE. *The foot of the bed which occupies most of the room can be seen, and that is all except that the walls are unpainted pine boards.* TYRONE *continues to stare at nothing, but becomes restless. His hands and mouth twitch.*

TYRONE (*suddenly with intense hatred*). You rotten bastard! (*He springs to his feet – fumbles in his pockets for cigarettes – strikes a match which lights up his face, on which there is now an expression of miserable guilt. His hand is trembling so violently he cannot light the cigarette.*)

Curtain.

ACT THREE

Scene. The living room wall has been replaced and all we see now of its lighted interior is through the two windows. Otherwise, everything is the same, and this Act follows the preceding without any lapse of time.

TYRONE is still trying with shaking hands to get his cigarette lighted. Finally he succeeds, and takes a deep inhale, and starts pacing back and forth a few steps, as if in a cell of his own thought. He swears defensively.

TYRONE. God damn it. You'll be crying in your beer in a minute. (*He begins to sing sneeringly half under his breath a snatch from an old sob song, popular in the Nineties.*)

> And baby's cries can't waken her
> In the baggage coach ahead.

(*His sneer changes to a look of stricken guilt and grief.*) Christ! (*He seems about to break down and sob but he fights this back.*) Cut it out, you drunken fool!

JOSIE can be seen through the windows, returning from the kitchen. He turns with a look of relief and escape.

Thank God!

He sits on the boulder and waits. JOSIE stops by the table in the living room to turn down the lamp until only a dim light remains. She has a quart of whiskey under her arm, two tumblers, and a pitcher of water. She goes through her bedroom and appears in the outer doorway. TYRONE gets up.

Ah! At last the old booze! (*He relieves her of the pitcher and tumblers as she comes down the steps.*)

JOSIE (*with a fixed smile*). You'd think I'd been gone years. You didn't seem so perishing for a drink.

TYRONE (*in his usual, easy, kidding way*). It's you I was perishing for. I've been dying of loneliness –

JOSIE. You'll die of lying some day. But I'm glad you're alive again. I thought when I left you really were dying on me.

TYRONE. No such luck.

JOSIE. Och, don't talk like that. Come and have a drink. We'll use the boulder for a table and I'll be bar-keep. (*He puts the pitcher and tumblers on the boulder and she uncorks the bottle. She takes a quick glance at his face – startledly.*) What's come over you, Jim? You look as if you've seen a ghost.

TYRONE (*looks away – dryly*). I have. My own. He's punk company.

JOSIE. Yes, it's the worst ghost of all, your own. Don't I know? But this will keep it in its place. (*She pours a tumbler half full of whiskey and hands it to him.*) Here. But wait till I join you. (*She pours the other tumbler half full.*)

TYRONE (*surprised*). Hello! I thought you never touched it.

JOSIE (*glibly*). I have on occasion. And this is one. I don't want to be left out altogether from celebrating our victory over Harder. (*She gives him a sharp bitter glance. Meeting his eyes, which are regarding her with puzzled wonder, she forces a laugh.*) Don't look at me as if I was up to some game. A drink or two will make me better company, and help me enjoy the moon and the night with you. Here's luck. (*She touches his glass with hers.*)

TYRONE (*shrugs his shoulders*). All right. Here's luck.

They drink. She gags and sputters. He pours water in her glass. She drinks it. He puts his glass and the pitcher back on the boulder. He keeps staring at her with a puzzled frown.

JOSIE. Some of it went down the wrong way.

TYRONE. So I see. That'll teach you to pour out baths instead of drinks.

JOSIE. It's the first time I ever heard you complain a drink was too big.

TYRONE. Yours was too big.

JOSIE. I'm my father's daughter. I've a strong head. So don't worry I'll pass out and you'll have to put me to bed. (*She gives a little bold laugh.*) Sure, that's a beautiful notion. I'll have to pretend I'm –

TYRONE (*irritably*). Nix on the raw stuff, Josie. Remember you said –

JOSIE (*resentment in her kidding*). I'd be different? That's right. I'm forgetting it's your pleasure to have me pretend I'm an innocent virgin tonight.

TYRONE (*in a strange tone that is almost threatening*). If you don't look out, I'll call you on that bluff, Josie. (*He stares at her with a deliberate sensualist's look that undresses her.*) I'd like to. You know that, don't you?

JOSIE (*boldly*). I don't at all. You're the one who's bluffing.

TYRONE (*grabs her in his arms – with genuine passion*). Josie! (*Then as suddenly he lets her go.*) Nix. Let's cut it out. (*He turns away. Her face betrays the confused conflict within her of fright, passion, happiness, and bitter resentment. He goes on with an abrupt change of tone.*) How about another drink? That's honest-to-God old bonded Bourbon. How the devil did Phil get hold of it?

JOSIE. Tom Lombardo, the bootlegger, gave him a case for letting him hide a truckload in our barn when the agents were after him. He stole it from a warehouse on faked permits. (*She pours out drinks as she speaks, a half tumblerful for him, a small one for herself.*) Here you are. (*She gives him his drink – smiles at him coquettishly, beginning to show the effect of her big drink by her increasingly bold manner.*) Let's sit down where the moon will be in our eyes and we'll see romance. (*She takes his arm and leads him to her bedroom steps. She sits on the top step, pulling him down beside her but on the one below. She raises her glass.*) Here's hoping before the night's out you'll have more courage and kiss me at least.

TYRONE (*frowns – then kiddingly*). That's a promise. Here's how. (*He drains his tumbler. She drinks half of hers. He puts his glass on the ground beside him. A pause. She tries to read his face without his noticing. He seems to be lapsing again into vague preoccupation.*)

JOSIE. Now don't sink back half-dead-and-alive in dreams the way you were before.

TYRONE (*quickly*). I'm not. I had a good final dose of heebie-jeebies when you were in the house. That's all for tonight. (*He adds a bit maudlinly, his two big drinks beginning to affect him.*) Let the dead past bury its dead.

JOSIE. That's the talk. There's only tonight, and the moon, and us – and the bonded Bourbon. Have another drink, and don't wait for me.

TYRONE. Not now, thanks. They're coming too fast. (*He gives her a curious, cynically amused look.*) Trying to get me soused, Josie?

JOSIE (*starts – quickly*). I'm not. Only to get you feeling happy, so you'll forget all sadness.

TYRONE (*kiddingly*). I might forget all my honourable intentions too. So look out.

JOSIE. I'll look forward to it – and I hope that's another promise, like the kiss you owe me. If you're suspicious I'm trying to get you soused – well, here goes. (*She drinks what is left in her glass.*) There, now. I must be scheming to get myself soused, too.

TYRONE. Maybe you are.

JOSIE (*resentfully*). If I was, it'd be to make you feel at home. Don't all the pretty little Broadway tarts get soused with you?

TYRONE (*irritably*). There you go again with that old line!

JOSIE. All right, I won't! (*Forcing a laugh.*) I must be eaten up with jealousy for them, that's it.

TYRONE. You needn't be. They don't belong.

JOSIE. And I do?

TYRONE. Yes. You do.

JOSIE. For tonight only, you mean?

TYRONE. We've agreed there is only tonight – and it's to be different from any past night – for both of us.

JOSIE (*in a forced, kidding tone*). I hope it will be. I'll try to control my envy for your Broadway flames. I suppose it's because I have a picture of them in my mind as small and dainty and pretty –

TYRONE. They're just gold-digging tramps.

JOSIE (*as if he hadn't spoken*). While I'm only a big, rough, ugly cow of a woman.

TYRONE. Shut up! You're beautiful.

JOSIE (*jeeringly, but her voice trembles*). God pity the blind!

TYRONE. You're beautiful to me.

JOSIE. It must be the Bourbon –

TYRONE. You're real and healthy and clean and fine and warm and strong and kind –

JOSIE. I have a beautiful soul, you mean?

TYRONE. Well, I don't know much about ladies' souls – (*He takes her hand.*) But I do know you're beautiful. (*He kisses her hand.*) And I love you a lot – in my fashion.

JOSIE (*stammers*). Jim – (*Hastily forcing her playful tone.*) Sure, you're full of fine compliments all of a sudden, and I ought to show you how pleased I am. (*She pulls his head back and kisses him on the lips – a quick, shy kiss.*) That's for my beautiful soul.

TYRONE (*the kiss arouses his pysical desire. He pulls her head down and stares into her eyes*). You have a beautiful strong body, too, Josie – and beautiful eyes and hair, and a beautiful smile and beautiful warm breasts. (*He kisses her on the lips. She pulls back frightenedly for a second – then returns his kiss. Suddenly he breaks away – in a tone of guilty irritation.*) Nix! Nix! Don't be a fool, Josie. Don't let me pull that stuff.

JOSIE (*triumphant for a second*). You meant it! I know you meant it! (*Then with resentful bitterness – roughly.*) Be God, you're right I'm a damned fool to let you make me forget you're the greatest liar in the world! (*Quickly.*) I mean, the greatest kidder. And now, how about another drink?

TYRONE (*staring at nothing vaguely*). You don't get me, Josie. You don't know – and I hope you never will know –

JOSIE (*blurts out bitterly*). Maybe I know more than you think.

TYRONE (*as if she hadn't spoken*). There's always the aftermath that poisons you. I don't want you to be poisoned –

JOSIE. Maybe you know what you're talking about –

TYRONE. And I don't want to be poisoned myself – not again – not with you. (*He pauses – slowly.*) There have been too many nights – and dawns. This must be different. I want – (*His voice trails off into silence.*)

JOSIE (*trying to read his face – uneasily*). Don't get in one of your queer spells, now. (*She gives his shoulder a shake – forcing a light tone.*) Sure, I don't think you know what you want. Except another drink. I'm sure you want that. And I want one, too.

TYRONE (*recovering himself*). Fine! Grand idea. (*He gets up and brings the bottle from the boulder. He picks up his tumbler and pours a big drink. She is holding out her tumbler but he ignores it.*)

JOSIE. You're not polite, pouring your own first.

TYRONE. I said a drink was a grand idea – for me. Not for you. You skip this one.

JOSIE (*resentfully*). Oh, I do, do I? Are you giving me orders?

TYRONE. Yes. Take a big drink of moonlight instead.

JOSIE (*angrily*). You'll pour me a drink, if you please, Jim Tyrone, or –

TYRONE (*stares at her – then shrugs his shoulders*). All right, if you want to take it that way, Josie. It's your funeral! (*He pours a drink into her tumbler.*)

JOSIE (*ashamed but defiant – stiffly*). Thank you kindly. (*She raises her glass – mockingly.*) Here's to tonight.

TYRONE *is staring at her, a strange bitter disgust in his eyes. Suddenly he slaps at her hand, knocking the glass to the ground.*

TYRONE (*his voice hard with repulsion*). I've slept with drunken tramps on too many nights!

JOSIE (*stares at him, too startled and bewildered to be angry. Her voice trembles with surprising meekness*). All right, Jim, if you don't want me to –

TYRONE (*now looks as bewildered by his action as she does*). I'm sorry, Josie. Don't know what the drink got into me. (*He picks up her glass.*) Here. I'll pour you another.

JOSIE (*still meek*). No, thank you. I'll skip this one. (*She puts her glass on the ground.*) But you drink up.

TYRONE. Thanks. (*He gulps down his drink. Mechanically, as if he didn't know what he was doing, he pours another. Suddenly he blurts out with guilty loathing.*) That fat blonde pig on the train – I got her drunk! That's why – (*He stops guiltily.*)

JOSIE (*uneasily*). What are you talking about? What train?

TYRONE. No train. Don't mind me. (*He gulps down the drink and pours another with the same strange air of acting unconsciously.*) Maybe I'll tell you – later, when I'm – That'll cure you – for all time! (*Abruptly he realises what he is saying. He gives the characteristic shrug of shoulders – cynically.*) Nuts! The Brooklyn boys are talking again. I guess I'm more stewed than I thought – in the centre of the old bean, at least. (*Dully.*) I better beat it back to the Inn and go to bed and stop bothering you, Josie.

JOSIE (*bullyingly – and pityingly*). Well, you won't, not if I have to hold you. Come on now, bring your drink and sit down like you were before. (*He does so. She pats his cheek – forcing a playful air.*) That's a good boy. And I won't take any more whiskey. I've all the effect from it I want already. Everything is far away and doesn't matter – except the moon and its dreams, and I'm part of the dreams – and you are, too. (*She adds with a rueful little laugh.*) I keep forgetting the thing I've got to remember. I keep hoping it's a lie, even though I know I'm a damned fool.

TYRONE (*hazily*). Damned fool about what?

JOSIE. Never mind. (*Forcing a laugh.*) I've just had a thought. If my poor old father had seen you knocking his prize whiskey on the ground – Holy Joseph, he'd have had three paralytic strokes!

TYRONE (*grins*). Yes, I can picture him. (*He pauses – with amused affection.*) But that's all a fake. He loves to play tightwad, but the people he likes know better. He'd give them his shirt. He's a grand old scout, Josie. (*A bit maudlin.*) The only real friend I've got left – except you. I love his guts.

JOSIE (*tensely – sickened by his hypocrisy*). Och, for the love of God –

TYRONE (*shrugs his shoulders*). Yes, I suppose that does sound like moaning-at-the-bar stuff . . . But I mean it.

JOSIE. Do you? Well, I know my father's virtues without you telling me.

TYRONE. You ought to appreciate him because he worships the ground you walk on – and he knows you a lot better than you think. (*He turns to smile at her teasingly.*) As well as I do – almost.

JOSIE (*defensively*). That's not saying much. Maybe I can guess what you think you know – (*Forcing a contemptuous laugh.*) If it's that, God pity you, you're a terrible fool.

TYRONE (*teasingly*). If it's what? I haven't said anything.

JOSIE. You'd better not, or I'll die laughing at you. (*She changes the subject abruptly.*) Why don't you drink up? It makes me nervous watching you hold it as if you didn't know it was there.

TYRONE. I didn't, at that. (*He drinks.*)

JOSIE. And have another.

TYRONE (*a bit drunkenly*). Will a whore go to a picnic? Real bonded Bourbon. That's my dish. (*He goes to the boulder for the bottle. He is as steady on his feet as if he were completely sober.*)

JOSIE (*in a light tone*). Bring the bottle back so it'll be handy and you won't have to leave me. I miss you.

TYRONE (*comes back with the bottle. He smiles at her cynically*). Still trying to get me soused, Josie?

JOSIE. I'm not such a fool – with your capacity.

TYRONE. You better watch your step. It might work – and then think of how disgusted you'd feel, with me lying beside you, probably snoring, as you watched the dawn come. You don't know –

JOSIE (*defiantly*). The hell I don't! Isn't that the way I've felt with every one of them, after?

TYRONE (*as if he hadn't heard – bitterly*). But take it from me, I know. I've seen too God-damned many dawns creeping greyly over too many dirty windows.

JOSIE (*ignores this – boldly*). But it might be different with you. Love could make it different. And I've been head over heels in love ever since you said you loved my beautiful soul. (*Again he doesn't seem to have heard – resentfully.*) Don't stand there like a loon, mourning over the past. Why don't you pour yourself a drink and sit down?

TYRONE (*looks at the bottle and tumbler in his hands, as if he'd forgotten them – mechanically*). Sure thing. Real bonded Bourbon. I ought to know. If I had a dollar for every drink of it I had before Prohibition, I'd hire our dear bully, Harder, for a valet.

JOSIE *stiffens and her face hardens.* TYRONE *pours a drink and sets the bottle on the ground. He looks up suddenly into her eye – warningly.*

You'd better remember I said you had beautiful eyes and hair – and breasts.

JOSIE. I remember you did. (*She tries to be calculatingly enticing.*) So sit down and I'll let you lay your head –

TYRONE. No. If you won't watch your step, I've got to. (*He sits down but doesn't lean back.*) And don't let me get away with pretending I'm so soused I don't know what I'm doing. I always know. Or part of me does. That's the trouble. (*He pauses – then bursts out in a strange threatening tone.*) You better look out, Josie. She was tickled to death to get me pie-eyed. Had an idea she could roll me, I guess. She wasn't so tickled about it – later on.

JOSIE. What she? (*He doesn't reply. She forces a light tone.*) I hope you don't think I'm scheming to roll you.

TYRONE (*vaguely*). What? (*Coming to – indignantly.*) Of course not. What are you talking about? For God's sake, you're not a tart.

JOSIE (*roughly*). No, I'm a fool. I'm always giving it away.

TYRONE (*angrily*). That lousy bluff again, eh? You're a liar! For Christ sake, quit the smut stuff, can't you!

JOSIE (*stung*). Listen to me, Jim! Drunk or not, don't you talk that way to me or –

TYRONE. How about your not talking the old smut stuff to me? You promised you'd be yourself. (*Pauses – vaguely.*) You don't get it, Josie. You see, she was one of the smuttiest talking pigs I've ever listened to.

JOSIE. What she? Do you mean the blonde on the train?

TYRONE (*starts – sharply*). Train? Who told you – ? (*Quickly.*) Oh – that's right – I did say – (*Vaguely.*) What blonde? What's the difference? Coming back from the Coast. It was long ago. But it seems like tonight. There is no present or future – only the past happening over and over again – now. You can't get away from it. (*Abruptly.*) Nuts! To hell with that crap.

JOSIE. You came back from the Coast about a year ago after – (*She checks herself.*)

TYRONE (*dully*). Yes. After Mama's death. (*Quickly.*) But I've been to the Coast a lot of times during my career as a third-rate ham. I don't remember which time – or anything much – except I was pie-eyed in a drawing room the whole four days. (*Abruptly.*) What were we talking about before? What a grand guy Phil is. You ought to be glad you've got him for a father. Mine was an old bastard.

JOSIE. He wasn't! He was one of the finest, kindest gentlemen ever lived.

TYRONE (*sneeringly*). Outside the family, sure. Inside, he was a lousy tightwad bastard.

JOSIE (*repelled*). You ought to be ashamed!

TYRONE. To speak ill of the dead? Nuts! He can't hear, and he knows I hated him, anyway – as much as he hated me. I'm glad he's dead. So is he. Or he ought to be. Everyone ought to be, if they have any sense. Out of a bum racket. At peace. (*He shrugs his shoulders.*) Nuts! What of it?

JOSIE (*tensely*). Don't, Jim. I hate you when you talk like that. (*Forcing a light tone.*) Do you want to spoil our beautiful moonlight night? And don't be telling me of your old flames, on trains or not. I'm too jealous.

TYRONE (*with a shudder of disgust*). Of that pig? (*He drinks his whiskey as if to wash a bad taste from his mouth – then takes one of her hands in both of his – simply.*) You're a fool to be jealous of anyone. You're the only woman I care a damn about.

JOSIE (*deeply stirred, in spite of herself – her voice trembling*). Jim, don't – (*Forcing a tense little laugh.*) All right, I'll try and believe that – for tonight.

TYRONE (*simply*). Thanks, Josie. (*A pause. He speaks in a tone of random curiosity.*) Why did you say a while ago I'd be leaving for New York soon?

JOSIE (*stiffens – her face hardening*). Well, I was right, wasn't I? (*Unconsciously she tries to pull her hand away.*)

TYRONE. Why are you pulling your hand away?

JOSIE (*stops*). Was I? (*Forcing a smile.*) I suppose because it seems crazy for you to hold my big ugly paw so tenderly. But you're welcome to it, if you like.

TYRONE. I do like. It's strong and kind and warm – like you. (*He kisses it.*)

JOSIE (*tensely*). Och, for the love of God – ! (*She jerks her hand away – then hastily forces a joking tone.*) Wasting kisses on my hand! Sure, even the moon is laughing at us.

TYRONE. Nuts for the moon! I'd rather have one light on Broadway than all the moons since Rameses was a pup. (*He takes cigarettes from his pocket and lights one.*)

JOSIE (*her eyes searching his face, lighted up by the match*). You'll be taking a train back to your dear old Broadway tomorrow night, won't you?

TYRONE (*still holding the burning match, stares at her in surprise*). Tomorrow night? Where did you get that?

JOSIE. A little bird told me.

TYRONE (*blows out the match in a cloud of smoke*). You'd better give that bird the bird. By the end of the week, is the right dope. Phil got his dates mixed.

JOSIE (*quickly*). He didn't tell me. He was too drunk to remember anything.

TYRONE. He was sober when I told him. I called up the executors when we reached the Inn after leaving here. They said the estate would be out of probate within a few days. I told Phil the glad tidings and bought drinks for all and sundry. There was quite a celebration. Funny, Phil wouldn't remember that.

JOSIE (*bewildered – not knowing what to believe*). It is – funny.

TYRONE (*shrugs his shoulders*). Well, he's stewed to the ears. That always explains anything. (*Then strangely.*) Only sometimes it doesn't.

JOSIE. No – sometimes it doesn't.

TYRONE (*goes on without real interest, talking to keep from thinking*). Phil certainly has a prize bun on tonight. He never took a punch at me before. And that drivel he talked about owing me one – What got into his head, I wonder.

JOSIE (*tensely*). How would I know, if you don't?

TYRONE. Well, I don't. Not unless – I remember I did try to get his goat. Simpson sat down with us. Harder sent him to see me. You remember after Harder left here I said the joke was on you, that you'd made this place a goldmine. I was kidding, but I had the right dope. What do you think he told Simpson to offer? Ten grand! On the level, Josie.

JOSIE (*tense*). So you accepted?

TYRONE. I told Simpson to tell Harder I did. I decided the best way to fix him was to let him think he'd got away with it, and then when he comes tomorrow morning to drive me to the executors' office, I'll tell him what he can do with himself, his bankroll, and tin oil tanks.

JOSIE (*knows he is telling the truth – so relieved she can only stammer stupidly*). So that's – the truth of it.

TYRONE (*smiles*). Of course, I did it to kid Phil, too. He was right there, listening. But I know I didn't fool him.

JOSIE (*weakly*). Maybe you did fool him, for once. But I don't know.

TYRONE. And that's why he took a swing at me? (*He laughs, but there is a forced note to it.*) Well, if so, it's one hell of a joke on him. (*His tone becomes hurt and bitter.*) All the same, I'll be good and sore, Josie. I promised this place wouldn't be sold except to him. What the hell does he think I am? He ought to know I wouldn't doublecross you and him for ten million!

JOSIE (*giving way at last to her relief and joy*). Don't I know! Oh, Jim, darling! (*She hugs him passionately and kisses him on the lips.*) I knew you'd never – I told him – (*She kisses him again.*) Oh, Jim, I love you.

TYRONE (*again with a strange, simple gratitude*). Thanks, Josie. I mean, for not believing I'm a rotten louse. Everyone else believes it – including myself – for a damned good reason. (*Abruptly changing the subject.*) I'm a fool to let this stuff about Phil get under my skin, but – Why, I remember telling him tonight I'd even written my brother and got his okay on selling the farm to him. And Phil thanked me. He seemed touched and grateful. You wouldn't think he'd forget that.

JOSIE (*her face hard and bitter*). I wouldn't, indeed. There's a lot of things he'll have to explain when he comes at sun – (*Hastily.*) When he comes back. (*She pauses – then bursts out.*) The damned old schemer, I'll teach him to – (*Again checking herself.*) to act like a fool.

TYRONE (*smiles*). You'll get out the old club, eh? What a bluff you are, Josie. (*Teasingly.*) You and your lovers, Messalina – when you've never –

JOSIE (*with a faint spark of her old defiance*). You're a liar.

TYRONE. 'Pride is the sin by which the angels fell.' Are you going to keep that up – with me?

JOSIE (*feebly*). You think I've never because no one would – because I'm a great ugly cow –

TYRONE (*gently*). Nuts! You could have had any one of them. You kidded them till you were sure they wanted you. That was all you wanted. And then you slapped them groggy when they tried for more. But you had to keep convincing yourself –

JOSIE (*tormentedly*). Don't, Jim.

TYRONE. You can take the truth, Josie – from me. Because you and I belong to the same club. We can kid the world but we can't fool ourselves, like most people, no matter what we do – nor escape ourselves no matter where we run away. Whether it's the bottom of a bottle, or a South Sea Island, we'd find our own ghosts there waiting to greet us – 'sleepless with pale commemorative eyes,' as Rossetti wrote. (*He sneers to himself.*) The old poetic bull, eh? Crap! (*Reverting to a teasing tone.*) You don't ask how I saw through your bluff, Josie. You pretend too much. And so do the guys. I've listened to them at the Inn. They all lie to each other. No one wants to admit all he got was a slap in the puss, when he thinks a lot of other guys made it. You can't blame them. And they know you don't give a damn how they lie. So –

JOSIE. For the love of God, Jim! Don't!

TYRONE. Phil is wise to you, of course, but although he knew I knew, he would never admit it until tonight.

JOSIE (*startled – vindictively*). So he admitted it, did he? Wait till I get hold of him!

TYRONE. He'll never admit it to you. He's afraid of hurting you.

JOSIE. He is, is he? Well – (*Almost hysterically.*) For the love of God, can't you shut up about him!

TYRONE (*glances up at her, surprised – then shrugs his shoulders*). Oh, all right. I wanted to clear things up, that's all – for Phil's sake as well as yours. You have a hell of a licence to be sore. He's the one who ought to be. Don't you realise what a lousy position you've put him in with your brazen-trollop act?

JOSIE (*tensely*). No. He doesn't care, except to use me in his scheming. He –

TYRONE. Don't be a damned fool. Of course he cares. And so do I. (*He turns and pulls her head down and kisses her on the lips.*) I care, Josie. I love you.

JOSIE (*with pitiful longing*). Do you, Jim? Do you? (*She forces a trembling smile – faintly.*) Then I'll confess the truth to you. I've been a crazy fool. I am a virgin. (*She begins to sob with a strange forlorn shame and humiliation.*) And now you'll never – and I want you – now more than ever – because I love you more than ever, after what's happened – (*Suddenly she kisses him with fierce passion.*) But you will! I'll make you! To hell with your

honourable scruples! I know you want me! I couldn't believe
that until tonight – but now I know. It's in your kisses! (*She
kisses him again – with passionate tenderness.*) Oh, you great fool!
As if I gave a damn what happened after! I'll have had tonight
and your love to remember for the rest of my days! (*She kisses
him again.*) Oh, Jim, darling, haven't you said yourself there's
only tonight? (*She whispers tenderly.*) Come. Come with me. (*She
gets to her feet, pulling at his arm – with a little self-mocking laugh.*)
But I'll have to make you leave before sunrise. I mustn't forget
that.

TYRONE (*a strange change has come over his face. He looks her over
now with a sneering cynical lust. He speaks thickly as if he was
suddenly very drunk*). Sure thing, Kiddo. What the hell else do
you suppose I came for? I've been kidding myself. (*He steps up
beside her and puts his arm round her and presses his body to hers.*)
You're the goods, Kid. I've wanted you all along. Love, nuts!
I'll show you what love is. I know what you want, Bright Eyes.
(*She is staring at him now with a look of frightened horror. He kisses
her roughly.*) Come on, Baby Doll, let's hit the hay. (*He pushes her
back in the doorway.*)

JOSIE (*strickenly*). Jim! Don't! (*She pulls his arms away so violently
that he staggers back and would fall down the steps if she didn't grab
his arm in time. As it is he goes down on one knee. She is on the verge
of collapse herself – brokenly.*) Jim! I'm not a whore.

TYRONE (*remains on one knee – confusedly, as if he didn't know what
had happened*). What the hell? Was I trying to rape you, Josie?
Forget it. I'm drunk – not responsible. (*He gets to his feet,
staggering a bit, and steps down to the ground.*)

JOSIE (*covering her face with her hands*). Oh, Jim! (*She sobs.*)

TYRONE (*with vague pity*). Don't cry. No harm done. You
stopped me, didn't you? (*She continues to sob. He mutters vaguely,
as if talking to himself.*) Must have drawn a blank for a while.
Nuts! Cut out the faking. I knew what I was doing. (*Slowly,
staring before him.*) But it's funny. I *was* seeing things. That's the
truth, Josie. For a moment I thought you were that blonde pig
– (*Hastily.*) The old heebie-jeebies. Hair of the dog. (*He gropes
around for the bottle and his glass.*) I'll have another shot –

JOSIE (*takes her hands from her face – fiercely*). Pour the whole
bottle down your throat, if you like! Only stop talking! (*She
covers her face with her hands and sobs again.*)

TYRONE (*stares at her with a hurt and sad expression – dully*). Can't forgive me, eh? You ought to. You ought to thank me for letting you see – (*He pauses, as if waiting for her to say something, but she remains silent. He shrugs his shoulders, pours out a big drink mechanically.*) Well, here's how. (*He drinks and puts the bottle and glass on the ground – dully.*) That was a nightcap. Our moonlight romance seems to be a flop, Josie. I guess I'd better go.

JOSIE (*dully*). Yes. You'd better go. Good night.

TYRONE. Not good night. Goodbye.

JOSIE (*lifts her head*). Goodbye?

TYRONE. Yes. I won't see you again before I leave for New York. I was a damned fool to come tonight. I hoped – But you don't get it. How could you? So what's the good – (*He shrugs his shoulders hopelessly and turns toward the road.*)

JOSIE. Jim!

TYRONE (*turning back – bitter accusation in his tone now*). Whore? Who said you were a whore? But I warned you, didn't I, if you kept on – Why did you have to act like one, asking me to come to bed? That wasn't what I came here for. And you promised tonight would be different. Why the hell did you promise that, if all you wanted was what all the others want, if that's all love means to you? (*Then guiltily.*) Oh, Christ, I don't mean that, Josie. I know how you feel, and if I could give you happiness – But it wouldn't work. You don't know me. I'd poison it for myself and for you. I've poisoned it already, haven't I, but it would be a million times worse after – No matter how I tried not to, I'd make it like all the other nights – for you, too. You'd lie awake and watch the dawn come with disgust, with nausea retching your memory, and the wine of passion poets blab about, a sour aftertaste in your mouth of Dago red ink! (*He gives a sneering laugh.*)

JOSIE (*distractedly*). Oh, Jim, don't! Please don't!

TYRONE. You'd hate me and yourself – not for a day or two but for the rest of your life. (*With a perverse, jeering note of vindictive boastfulness in his tone.*) Believe me, Kid, when I poison them, they stay poisoned!

JOSIE (*with dull bitterness*). Goodbye, Jim.

TYRONE (*miserably hurt and sad for a second – appealingly*). Josie – (*Gives the characteristic shrug of his shoulders – simply.*) Goodbye.

(*He turns toward the road – bitterly.*) I'll find it hard to forgive, too. I came here asking for love – just for this one night – because I thought you loved me. (*Dully.*) Nuts. To hell with it. (*He starts away.*)

JOSIE (*watches him for a second, fighting the love that, in spite of her, responds to his appeal – then she springs up and runs to him – with fierce, possessive, maternal tenderness*). Come here to me, you great fool, and stop your silly blather. There's nothing to hate you for. There's nothing to forgive. Sure, I was only trying to give you happiness, because I love you. I'm sorry I was so stupid and didn't see – But I see now, and you'll find I have all the love you need. (*She gives him a hug and kisses him. There is passion in her kiss but it is a tender, protective maternal passion, which he responds to with an instant grateful yielding.*)

TYRONE (*simply*). Thanks, Josie. You're beautiful. I love you. I knew you'd understand.

JOSIE. Of course I do. Come, now. (*She leads him back, her arm around his waist.*)

TYRONE. I didn't want to leave you. You know that.

JOSIE. Indeed I know it. Come now. We'll sit down. (*She sits on the top step and pulls him down on the step below her.*) That's it – with my arm around you. Now lay your head on my breast – the way you said you wanted to do – (*He lets his head fall back on her breast. She hugs him – gently.*) There, now. Forget all about my being a fool and forgive – (*Her voice trembles – but she goes on determinedly.*) Forgive my selfishness, thinking only of myself. Sure, if there's one thing I owe you tonight, after all my lying and scheming, it's to give you the love you need, and it'll be my pride and my joy – (*Forcing a trembling echo of her playful tone.*) It's easy enough, too, for I have all kinds of love for you – and maybe this is the greatest of all – because it costs so much. (*She pauses, looking down at his face. He has closed his eyes and his haggard, dissipated face looks like a pale mask in the moonlight – at peace as a death mask is at peace. She becomes frightened.*) Jim! Don't look like that!

TYRONE (*opens his eyes – vaguely*). Like what?

JOSIE (*quickly*). It's the moonlight. It makes you look so pale, and with your eyes closed –

TYRONE (*simply*). You mean I looked dead?

JOSIE. No! As if you'd fallen asleep.

TYRONE (*speaks in a tired, empty tone, as if he felt he ought to explain something to her – something which no longer interests him*). Listen, and I'll tell you a little story, Josie. All my life I had just one dream. From the time I was a kid, I loved racehorses. I thought they were the most beautiful things in the world. I liked to gamble, too. So the big dream was that some day I'd have enough dough to play a cagey system of betting on favourites, and follow the horses south in the winter, and come back north with them in the spring, and be at the track every day. It seemed that would be the ideal life – for me. (*He pauses.*)

JOSIE. Well, you'll be able to do it.

TYRONE. No. I won't be able to do it, Josie. That's the joke. I gave it a tryout before I came up here. I borrowed some money on my share of the estate and started going to tracks. But it didn't work. I played my system, but I found I didn't care if I won or lost. The horses were beautiful, but I found myself saying to myself, what of it? Their beauty didn't mean anything. I found that every day I was glad when the last race was over, and I could go back to the hotel – and the bottle in my room. (*He pauses, staring into the moonlight with vacant eyes.*)

JOSIE (*uneasily*). Why did you tell me this?

TYRONE (*in the same listless monotone*). You said I looked dead. Well, I am.

JOSIE. You're not! (*She hugs him protectively.*) Don't talk like that!

TYRONE. Ever since Mama died.

JOSIE (*deeply moved – pityingly*). I know. I've felt all along it was that sorrow was making you – (*She pauses – gently.*) Maybe if you talked about your grief for her, it would help you. I think it must be all choked up inside you, killing you.

TYRONE (*in a strange warning tone*). You'd better look out, Josie.

JOSIE. Why?

TYRONE (*quickly, forcing his cynical smile*). I might develop a crying jag, and sob on your beautiful breast.

JOSIE (*gently*). You can sob all you like.

TYRONE. Don't encourage me. You'd be sorry. (*A deep conflict shows in his expression and tone. He is driven to go on in spite of himself.*) But if you're such a glutton for punishment – After all, I said I'd tell you later, didn't I?

JOSIE (*puzzled*). You said you'd tell me about the blonde on the train.

TYRONE. She's part of it. I lied about that. (*He pauses – then blurts out sneeringly.*) You won't believe it could have happened. Or if you did believe, you couldn't understand or forgive – (*Quickly.*) But you might. You're the one person who might. Because you really love me. And because you're the only woman I've ever met who understands the lousy rotten things a man can do when he's crazy drunk, and draws a blank – especially when he's nutty with grief to start with.

JOSIE (*hugging him tenderly*). Of course I'll understand, Jim, darling.

TYRONE (*stares into the moonlight – hauntedly*). But I didn't draw a blank. I tried to. I drank enough to knock out ten men. But it didn't work. I knew what I was doing. (*He pauses – dully.*) No, I can't tell you, Josie. You'd loathe my guts, and I couldn't blame you.

JOSIE. No! I'll love you no matter what –

TYRONE (*with strange triumphant harshness*). All right! Remember that's a promise! (*He pauses – starts to speak – pauses again.*)

JOSIE (*pityingly*). Maybe you'd better not – if it will make you suffer.

TYRONE. Trying to welch now, eh? It's too late. You've got me started. Suffer? Christ, I ought to suffer! (*He pauses. Then he closes his eyes. It is as if he had to hide from sight before he can begin. He makes his face expressionless. His voice becomes impersonal and objective, as though what he told concerned some man he had known, but had nothing to do with him. This is the only way he can start telling the story.*) When Mama died, I'd been on the wagon for nearly two years. Not even a glass of beer. Honestly. And I know I would have stayed on. For her sake. She had no one but me. The Old Man was dead. My brother had married – had a kid – had his own life to live. She'd lost him. She had only me to attend to things for her and take care of her. She'd always hated my drinking. So I quit. It made me happy to do it. For her. Because she was all I had, all I cared about. Because I loved her. (*He pauses.*) No one would believe that now, who knew – But I did.

JOSIE (*gently*). I know how much you loved her.

TYRONE. We went out to the Coast to see about selling a piece of property the Old Man had bought there years ago. And one day she suddenly became ill. Got rapidly worse. Went into a coma. Brain tumour. The docs said, no hope. Might never come out of coma. I went crazy. Couldn't face losing her. The old booze yen got me. I got drunk and stayed drunk. And I began hoping she's never come out of the coma, and see I was drinking again. That was my excuse, too – that she'd never know. And she never did. (*He pauses – then sneeringly.*) Nix! Kidding myself again. I know damned well just before she died she recognised me. She saw I was drunk. Then she closed her eyes so she couldn't see, and was glad to die! (*He opens his eyes and stares into the moonlight as if he saw this deathbed scene before him.*)

JOSIE (*soothingly*). Ssshh. You only imagine that because you feel guilty about drinking.

TYRONE (*as if he hadn't heard, closes his eyes again*). After that, I kept so drunk I did draw a blank most of the time, but I went through the necessary motions and no one guessed how drunk – (*He pauses.*) But there are things I can never forget – the undertakers, and her body in a coffin with her face made up. I couldn't hardly recognise her. She looked young and pretty like someone I remembered meeting long ago. Practically a stranger. To whom I was a stranger. Cold and indifferent. Not worried about me any more. Free at last. Free from worry. From pain. From me. I stood looking down at her, and something happened to me. I found I couldn't feel anything. I knew I ought to be heartbroken but I couldn't feel anything. I seemed dead, too. I knew I ought to cry. Even a crying jag would look better than just standing there. But I couldn't cry. I cursed to myself, 'You dirty bastard, it's Mama. You loved her, and now she's dead. She's gone away from you for ever. Never, never again –' But it had no effect. All I did was to try to explain to myself, 'She's dead. What does she care now if I cry or not, or what I do? It doesn't matter a damn to her. She's happy to be where I can't hurt her ever again. She's rid of me at last. For God's sake, can't you leave her alone even now? For God's sake, can't you let her rest in peace?' (*He pauses – then sneeringly.*) But there were several people around and I knew they expected me to show something. Once a ham, always a ham! So I put on an act. I flopped on my knees and hid my face in my hands and faked some sobs and cried, 'Mama! Mama! My dear mother!' But all the time I kept saying to myself, 'You lousy ham! You God-damned lousy ham! Christ, in a minute you'll start singing 'Mother Machree'!' (*He opens his eyes and gives a tortured, sneering laugh, staring into the moonlight.*)

JOSIE (*horrified, but still deeply pitying*). Jim! Don't! It's past. You've punished yourself. And you were drunk. You didn't mean –

TYRONE (*again closes his eyes*). I had to bring her body East to be buried beside the Old Man. I took a drawing room and hid in it with a case of booze. She was in her coffin in the baggage car. No matter how drunk I got, I couldn't forget that for a minute. I found I couldn't stay alone in the drawing room. It became haunted. I was going crazy. I had to go out and wander up and down the train looking for company. I made such a public nuisance of myself that the conductor threatened if I didn't quit, he'd keep me locked in the drawing room. But I'd spotted one passenger who was used to drunks and could pretend to like them, if there was enough dough in it. She had parlour house written all over her – a blonde pig who looked more like a whore than twenty-five whores, with a face like an overgrown doll's and a come-on smile as cold as a polar bear's feet. I bribed the porter to take a message to her and that night she sneaked into my drawing room. She was bound for New York, too. So every night – for fifty bucks a night – (*He opens his eyes and now he stares torturedly through the moonlight into the drawing room.*)

JOSIE (*her face full of revulsion – stammers*). Oh, how could you! (*Instinctively she draws away, taking her arms from around him.*)

TYRONE. How could I? I don't know. But I did. I suppose I had some mad idea she could make me forget – what was in the baggage car ahead.

JOSIE. Don't. (*She draws back again so he has to raise his head from her breast. He doesn't seem to notice this.*)

TYRONE. No, it couldn't have been that. Because I didn't seem to want to forget. It was like some plot I had to carry out. The blonde – she didn't matter. She was only something that belonged in the plot. It was as if I wanted revenge – because I'd been left alone – because I knew I was lost, without any hope left – that all I could do would be drink myself to death, because no one was left who could help me. (*His face hardens and a look of cruel vindictiveness comes into it – with a strange horrible satisfaction in his tone.*) No, I didn't forget even in that pig's arms! I remembered the last two lines of a lousy tearjerker song I'd heard when I was a kid kept singing over and over in my brain.

> And baby's cries can't waken her
> In the baggage coach ahead

JOSIE (*distractedly*). Jim!

TYRONE. I couldn't stop it singing. I didn't want to stop it!

JOSIE. Jim! For the love of God. I don't want to hear!

TYRONE (*after a pause – dully*). Well, that's all – except I was too drunk to go to her funeral.

JOSIE. Oh! (*She has drawn away from him as far as she can without getting up. He becomes aware of this for the first time and turns slowly to stare at her.*)

TYRONE (*dully*). Don't want to touch me now, eh? (*He shrugs his shoulders mechanically.*) Sorry. I'm a damned fool. I shouldn't have told you.

JOSIE (*her horror ebbing as her love and protective compassion returns – moves nearer him – haltingly*). Don't, Jim. Don't say – I don't want to touch you. It's – a lie. (*She puts a hand on his shoulder.*)

TYRONE (*as if she hadn't spoken – with hopeless longing*). Wish I could believe in the spiritualists' bunk. If I could tell her it was because I missed her so much and couldn't forgive her for leaving me –

JOSIE. Jim! For the love of God – !

TYRONE (*unheeding*). She'd understand and forgive me, don't you think? She always did. She was simple and kind and pure of heart. She was beautiful. You're like her deep in your heart. That's why I told you. I thought – (*Abruptly his expression becomes sneering and cynical – harshly.*) My mistake. Nuts! Forget it. Time I got a move on. I don't like your damned moon, Josie. It's an ad for the past. (*He recites mockingly.*)

> It is the very error of the moon:
> She comes more nearer earth than she was wont,
> And makes men mad.

(*He moves.*) I'll grab the last trolley for town. There'll be a speak open, and some drunk laughing. I need a laugh. (*He starts to get up.*)

JOSIE (*throws her arms around him and pulls him back – tensely*). No! you won't go! I won't let you! (*She hugs him close – gently.*) I understand now, Jim, darling, and I'm proud you came to me as the one in the world you know loves you enough to understand and forgive – and I do forgive!

TYRONE (*lets his head fall back on her breast – simply*). Thanks, Josie. I knew you –

JOSIE. And *she* forgives, do you hear me! As *she* loves and understands and forgives!

TYRONE (*simply*). Yes, I know she – (*His voice breaks.*)

JOSIE (*bends over him with a brooding maternal tenderness*). That's right. Do what you came for, my darling. It isn't drunken laughter in a speakeasy you want to hear at all, but the sound of yourself crying your heart's repentance against her breast. (*His face is convulsed. He hides it on her breast and sobs rackingly. She hugs him more tightly and speaks softly, staring into the moonlight.*) *She* hears. I feel her in the moonlight, her soul wrapped in it like a silver mantle, and I know she understands and forgives me, too, and her blessing lies on me. (*A pause. His sobs begin to stop exhaustedly. She looks down at him again and speaks soothingly as she would to a child.*) There. There, now. (*He stops. She goes on in a gentle, bullying tone.*) You're a fine one, wanting to leave me when the night I promised I'd give you has just begun, our night that'll be different from all the others, with a dawn that won't creep over dirty window-panes but will wake in the sky like a promise of God's peace in the soul's dark sadness. (*She smiles a little amused smile.*) Will you listen to me, Jim! I must be a poet. Who would have guessed it? Sure, love is a wonderful mad inspiration! (*A pause. She looks down. His eyes are closed. His face against her breast looks pale and haggard in the moonlight. Calm with the drained, exhausted peace of death. For a second she is frightened. Then she realises and whispers softly.*) Asleep. (*In a tender crooning tone like a lullaby.*) That's right. Sleep in peace, my darling. (*Then with sudden anguished longing.*) Oh, Jim, Jim, maybe my love could still save you, if you could want it enough! (*She shakes her head.*) No. That can never be. (*Her eyes leave his face to stare up at the sky. She looks weary and stricken and sad. She forces a defensive, self-derisive smile.*) God forgive me, it's a fine end to all my scheming, to sit here with the dead hugged to my breast, and the silly mug of the moon grinning down, enjoying the joke!

Curtain.

ACT FOUR

Scene. Same as Act Three. It is dawn. The first faint streaks of colour, heralding the sunrise, appear in the eastern sky at left.

JOSIE sits in the same position on the steps, as if she had not moved, her arms around TYRONE. He is still asleep, his head on her breast. His face has the same exhausted, death-like repose. JOSIE's face is set in an expression of numbed, resigned sadness. Her body sags tiredly. In spite of her strength, holding herself like this for hours, for fear of waking him, is becoming too much for her.

The two make a strangely tragic picture in the wan dawn light – this big sorrowful woman hugging a haggard-faced, middle-aged drunkard against her breast, as if he were a sick child.

HOGAN appears at left-rear, coming from the barn. He approaches the corner of the house stealthily on tiptoe. Wisps of hay stick to his clothes and his face is swollen and sleepy, but his little pig's eyes are sharply wide awake and sober. He peeks around the corner, and takes in the two on the steps. His eyes fix on JOSIE's face in a long, probing stare.

JOSIE (*speaks in a low grim tone*). Stop hiding, Father. I heard you sneak up.

> *He comes guiltily around the corner. She keeps her voice low, but her tone is commanding.*

Come here, and be quiet about it.

> *He obeys meekly, coming as far as the boulder silently, his eyes searching her face, his expression becoming guilty and miserable at what he sees. She goes on in the same tone, without looking at him.*

Talk low, now. I don't want him wakened – (*She adds strangely.*) Not until the dawn has beauty in it.

HOGAN (*worriedly*). What? (*He decides it's better for the present to ask no questions. His eyes fall on TYRONE's face. In spite of himself, he is startled – in an awed, almost frightened whisper.*) Be God, he looks dead!

JOSIE (*strangely*). Why wouldn't he? He is.

HOGAN. Is?

JOSIE. Don't be a fool. Can't you see him breathing? Dead asleep, I mean. Don't stand there gawking. Sit down.

He sits meekly on the boulder. His face betrays a guilty dread of what is coming. There is a pause in which she doesn't look at him but he keeps glancing at her, growing visibly more uneasy. She speaks bitterly.

Where's your witnesses?

HOGAN (*guiltily*). Witnesses? (*Then forcing an amused grin.*) Oh, bc God, if that ain't a joke on me! Sure, I got so blind drunk at the Inn I forgot all about our scheme and came home and went to sleep in the hayloft.

JOSIE (*her expression harder and more bitter*). You're a liar.

HOGAN. I'm not. I just woke up. Look at the hay sticking to me. That's proof.

JOSIE. I'm not thinking of that, and well you know it. (*With bitter voice.*) So you just woke up – did you? – and then came sneaking here to see if the scheme behind your scheme had worked!

HOGAN (*guiltily*). I don't know what you mean.

JOSIE. Don't lie any more, Father. This time, you've told one too many.

He starts to defend himself but the look on her face makes him think better of it and he remains uneasily silent. A pause.

HOGAN (*finally has to blurt out*). Sure, if I'd brought the witnesses, there's nothing for them to witness that –

JOSIE. No. You're right, there. There's nothing. Nothing at all. (*She smiles strangely.*) Except a great miracle they'd never believe, or you either.

HOGAN. What miracle?

JOSIE. A virgin who bears a dead child in the night, and the dawn finds her still a virgin. If that isn't a miracle, what is?

HOGAN (*uneasily*). Stop talking so queer. You give me the shivers. (*He attempts a joking tone.*) Is it you who's the virgin? Faith, that *would* be a miracle, no less! (*He forces a chuckle.*)

JOSIE. I told you to stop lying, Father.

HOGAN. What lie? (*He stops and watches her face worriedly. She is silent, as if she were not aware of him now. Her eyes are fixed on the wanton sky.*)

JOSIE (*as if to herself*). It'll be beautiful soon, and I can wake him.

HOGAN (*can't retain his anxiety any longer*). Josie, darlin'! For the love of God, can't you tell me what happened to you?

JOSIE (*her face hard and bitter again*). I've told you once. Nothing.

HOGAN. Nothing? If you could see the sadness in your face –

JOSIE. What woman doesn't sorrow for the man she loved who has died? But there's pride in my heart, too.

HOGAN (*tormentedly*). Will you stop talking as if you'd gone mad in the night! (*Raising his voice – with revengeful anger.*) Listen to me! If Jim Tyrone has done anything to bring you sorrow –

TYRONE *stirs in his sleep and moans, pressing his face against her breast as if for protection. She looks down at him and hugs him close.*

JOSIE (*croons softly*). There, there, my darling. Rest in peace a while longer. (*Turns on her father angrily and whispers.*) Didn't I tell you to speak low and not wake him! (*She pauses – then quietly.*) He did nothing to bring me sorrow. It was my mistake. I thought there was still hope. I didn't know he'd died already – that it was a damned soul coming to me in the moonlight, to confess and be forgiven and find peace for a night –

HOGAN. Josie! Will you stop!

JOSIE (*after a pause – dully*). He'd never do anything to hurt me. You know it. (*Self-mockingly.*) Sure, hasn't he told me I'm beautiful to him and he loves me – in his fashion. (*Then matter-of-factly.*) All that happened was that he got drunk and he had one of his crazy notions he wanted to sleep the way he is, and I let him sleep. (*With forced roughness.*) And, be God, the night's over. I'm half dead with tiredness and sleepiness. It's that you see in my face, not sorrow.

HOGAN. Don't try to fool me, Josie. I –

JOSIE (*her face hard and bitter – grimly*). Fool you, is it? It's you who made a fool of me with your lies, thinking you'd use me to get your dirty greasy paws on the money he'll have!

HOGAN. No! I swear by all the saints –

JOSIE. You'd swear on a Bible while you were stealing it! (*Grimly.*) Listen to me, Father. I didn't call you here to answer questions about what's none of your business. I called you here to tell you I've seen through all the lies you told last night to get me to – (*As he starts to speak.*) Shut up! I'll do the talking now. You weren't drunk. You were only putting it on as part of your scheme –

HOGAN (*quietly*). I wasn't drunk, no. I admit that, Josie. But I'd had slews of drinks and they were in my head or I'd never have the crazy dreams –

JOSIE (*with biting scorn*). Dreams, is it? The only dream you've ever had, or will have, is of yourself counting a fistful of dirty money, and divil a care how you got it, or who you robbed or made suffer!

HOGAN (*winces – pleadingly*). Josie!

JOSIE. Shut up. (*Scathingly.*) I'm sure you've made up a whole new set of lies and excuses. You're that cunning and clever, but you can save your breath. They wouldn't fool me now. I've been fooled once too often. (*He gives her a frightened look, as if something he had dreaded has happened. She goes on, grimly accusing.*) You lied about Jim selling the farm. You knew he was kidding. You knew the estate would be out of probate in a few days, and he'd go back to Broadway, and you had to do something quick or you'd lose the last chance of getting your greedy hooks on his money.

HOGAN (*miserably*). No. It wasn't that, Josie.

JOSIE. You saw how hurt and angry I was because he'd kept me waiting here, and you used that. You knew I loved him and wanted him and you used that. You used all you knew about me – Oh, you did it clever! You ought to be proud! You worked it so it was me who did all the dirty scheming – You knew I'd find out from Jim you'd lied about the farm, but not before your lie had done its work – made me go after him, get him drunk, get drunk myself so I could be shameless – and when the truth did come out, wouldn't it make me love him all the more and be more shameless and willing? Don't tell me you didn't count on that, and you such a clever schemer! And if he once had me, knowing I was a virgin, didn't you count on his honour and remorse, and his loving me in his fashion, to make him offer to marry me? Sure, why wouldn't he, you thought. It wouldn't hold him. He'd go back to Broadway just the same and never see me again. But there'd be money in it, and when he'd finished killing himself, I'd be his legal widow and get what's left.

HOGAN (*miserably*). No! It wasn't that.

JOSIE. But what's the good of talking? It's all over. I've only one more word for you, Father, and it's this: I'm leaving you today,

like my brothers left. You can live alone and work alone your
cunning schemes on yourself.

HOGAN (*after a pause – slowly*). I knew you'd be bitter against me,
Josie, but I took the chance you'd be so happy you wouldn't
care how –

JOSIE (*as if she hadn't heard, looking at the eastern sky which is now
glowing with colour*). Thank God, it's beautiful. It's time. (*To
HOGAN.*) Go in the house and stay there till he's gone. I don't
want you around to start some new scheme.

*He looks miserable, starts to speak, thinks better of it, and meekly tiptoes
past her up the steps and goes in, closing the door quietly after him. She
looks down at* TYRONE. *Her face softens with a maternal tenderness
– sadly.*

I hate to bring you back to life, Jim, darling. If you could have
died in your sleep, that's what you would have liked, isn't it?
(*She gives him a gentle shake.*) Wake up, Jim. (*He moans in his sleep
and presses more closely against her. She stares at his face.*) Dear God,
let him remember that one thing and forget the rest. That will
be enough for me. (*She gives him a more vigorous shake.*) Jim!
Wake up, do you hear? It's time.

TYRONE (*half wakens without opening his eyes – mutters*). What the
hell? (*Dimly conscious of a woman's body – cynically.*) Again, eh?
Same old stuff. Who the hell are you, sweetheart? (*Irritably.*)
What's the big idea, waking me up? What time is it?

JOSIE. It's dawn.

TYRONE (*still without opening his eyes*). Dawn? (*He quotes drowsily.*)

But I was desolate and sick of an old passion,
When I awoke and found the dawn was grey.

(*Then with a sneer.*) They're all grey. Go to sleep, Kid – and let
me sleep. (*He falls asleep again.*)

JOSIE (*tensely*). This one isn't grey, Jim. It's different from all the
others – (*She sees he is asleep – bitterly.*) He'll have forgotten. He'll
never notice. And I'm the whore on the train to him now, not –
(*Suddenly she pushes him away from her and shakes him roughly.*) Will
you wake up, for God's sake! I've had all I can bear –

TYRONE (*still half asleep*). Hey! Cut out the rough stuff, Kid.
What? (*Awake now, blinking his eyes – with dazed surprise.*) Josie.

JOSIE (*still bitter*). That's who, and none of your damned tarts!
(*She pushes him.*) Get up now, so you won't fall asleep again. (*He*

does so with difficulty, still in a sleepy daze, his body stiff and cramped. She conquers her bitter resentment and puts on her old free-and-easy kidding tone with him, but all the time waiting to see how much he will remember.) You're stiff and cramped, and no wonder. I'm worse from holding you, if that's any comfort. (*She stretches and rubs her numbed arms, groaning comically.*) Holy Joseph, I'm a wreck entirely. I'll never be the same. (*Giving him a quick glance.*) You look as if you'd drawn a blank and were wondering how you got here. I'll bet you don't remember a thing.

TYRONE (*moving his arms and legs gingerly – sleepily*). I don't know. Wait till I'm sure I'm still alive.

JOSIE. You need an eye-opener. (*She picks up the bottle and glass and pours him a drink.*) Here you are.

TYRONE (*takes the glass mechanically*). Thanks, Josie. (*He goes and sits on the boulder, holding the drink as if he had no interest in it.*)

JOSIE (*watching him*). Drink up or you'll be asleep again.

TYRONE. No, I'm awake now, Josie. Funny. Don't seem to want a drink. Oh, I've got a head all right. But no heebie-jeebies – yet.

JOSIE. That's fine. It must be a pleasant change –

TYRONE. It is. I've got a nice, dreamy peaceful hangover for once – as if I'd had a sound sleep without nightmares.

JOSIE. So you did. Divil a nightmare. I ought to know. Wasn't I holding you and keeping them away?

TYRONE. You mean you – (*Suddenly.*) Wait a minute. I remember now I was sitting alone at a table in the Inn, and I suddenly had a crazy notion I'd come up here and sleep with my head on your – So that's why I woke up in your arms. (*Shamefacedly.*) And you let me get away with it. You're a nut, Josie.

JOSIE. Oh, I didn't mind.

TYRONE. You must have seen how blotto I was, didn't you?

JOSIE. I did. You were as full as a tick.

TYRONE. Then why didn't you give me the bum's rush?

JOSIE. Why would I? I was glad to humour you.

TYRONE. For God's sake, how long was I cramped on you like that?

JOSIE. Oh, a few hours, only.

TYRONE. God, I'm sorry, Josie, but it's your own fault for letting me –

JOSIE. Och, don't be apologising. I was glad of the excuse to stay awake and enjoy the beauty of the moon.

TYRONE. Yes, I can remember what a beautiful night it was.

JOSIE. Can you? I'm glad of that, Jim. You seemed to enjoy it the while we were sitting here together before you fell asleep.

TYRONE. How long a while was that?

JOSIE. Not long. Less than an hour, anyway.

TYRONE. I suppose I bored the hell out of you with a lot of drunken drivel.

JOSIE. Not a lot, no. But some. You were full of blarney, saying how beautiful I was to you.

TYRONE (*earnestly*). That wasn't drivel, Josie. You were. You are. You always will be.

JOSIE. You're a wonder, Jim. Nothing can stop you, can it? Even me in the light of dawn, looking like something you'd put in the field to scare the crows from the corn. You'll kid at the Day of Judgment.

TYRONE (*impatiently*). You know damned well it isn't kidding. You're not a fool. You can tell.

JOSIE (*kiddingly*). All right, then, I'm beautiful and you love me – in your fashion.

TYRONE. 'In my fashion,' eh? Was I reciting poetry to you? That must have been hard to take.

JOSIE. It wasn't. I liked it. It was all about beautiful nights and the romance of the moon.

TYRONE. Well, there was some excuse for that, anyway. It sure was a beautiful night. I'll never forget it.

JOSIE. I'm glad, Jim.

TYRONE. What other bunk did I pull on you – or I mean, did old John Barleycorn pull?

JOSIE. Not much. You were mostly quiet and sad – in a kind of daze, as if the moon was in your wits as well as whiskey.

TYRONE. I remember I was having a grand time at the Inn, celebrating with Phil, and then suddenly, for no reason, all the fun went out of it, and I was more melancholy than ten Hamlets. (*He pauses.*) Hope I didn't tell you the sad story of my life and weep on your bosom, Josie.

JOSIE. You didn't. The one thing you talked a lot about was that you wanted the night with me to be different from all the other nights you'd spent with women.

TYRONE (*with revulsion*). God, don't make me think of those tramps now! (*Then with deep, grateful feeling.*) It sure was different, Josie. I may not remember much, but I know how different it was from the way I feel now. None of my usual morning-after stuff – the damned sick remorse that makes you wish you'd died in your sleep so you wouldn't have to face the rotten things you're afraid you said and did the night before, when you were so drunk you didn't know what you were doing.

JOSIE. There's nothing you said or did last night for you to regret. You can take my word for that.

TYRONE (*as if he hadn't heard – slowly*). It's hard to describe how I feel. It's a new one on me. Sort of at peace with myself and this lousy life – as if all my sins had been forgiven – (*He becomes self-conscious – cynically.*) Nuts with that sin bunk, but you know what I mean.

JOSIE (*tensely*). I do, and I'm happy you feel that way, Jim. (*A pause. She goes on.*) You talked about how you'd watched too many dawns come creeping greyly over dirty window-panes, with some tart snoring beside you –

TYRONE (*winces*). Have a heart. Don't remind me of that now, Josie. Don't spoil this dawn!

A pause. She watches him tensely. He turns slowly to face the east, where the sky is now glowing with all the colours of an exceptionally beautiful sunrise. He stares, drawing a deep breath. He is profoundly moved but immediately becomes self-conscious and tries to sneer it off – cynically.

God seems to be putting on quite a display. I like Belasco better. Rise of curtain, Act-Four stuff. (*Her face has fallen into lines of bitter hurt, but he adds quickly and angrily.*) God damn it! Why do I have to pull that lousy stuff? (*With genuine deep feeling.*) God, it's beautiful, Josie! I – I'll never forget it – here with you.

JOSIE (*her face clearing – simply*). I'm glad, Jim. I was hoping you'd feel beauty in it – by way of a token.

TYRONE (*watching the sunrise – mechanically*). Token of what?

JOSIE. Oh, I don't know. Token to me that – never mind. I forget what I meant. (*Abruptly changing the subject.*) Don't think I woke you just to admire the sunrise. You're on a farm, not Broadway, and it's time for me to start work, not to go to bed. (*She gets to her feet and stretches. There is a growing strain behind her free-and-easy manner.*) And that's a hint, Jim. I can't stay entertaining you. So go back to the Inn, that's a good boy. I know you'll understand the reason, and not think I'm tired of your company. (*She forces a smile.*)

TYRONE (*gets up*). Of course I understand. (*He pauses – then blurts out guiltily.*) One more question. You're sure I didn't get out of order last night – and try to make you, or anything like that.

JOSIE. You didn't. You kidded back when I kidded you, the way we always do. That's all.

TYRONE. Thank God for that. I'd never forgive myself if – I wouldn't have asked you except I've pulled some pretty rotten stuff when I was drawing a blank. (*He becomes conscious of the forgotten drink he has in his hand.*) Well, I might as well drink this. The bar at the Inn won't be open for hours. (*He drinks – then looks pleasantly surprised.*) I'll be damned! That isn't Phil's rotgut. That's real honest-to-God bonded Bourbon. Where –

This clicks in his mind and suddenly he remembers everything and JOSIE sees that he does. The look of guilt and shame and anguish settles over his face. Instinctively he throws the glass away, his first reaction one of loathing for the drink which brought back memory. He feels JOSIE staring at him and fights desperately to control his voice and expression.

Real Bourbon. I remember now you said a bootlegger gave it to Phil. Well, I'll run along and let you do your work. See you later, Josie. (*He turns toward the road.*)

JOSIE (*strickenly*). No! Don't, Jim! Don't go like that! You won't see me later. You'll never see me again now, and I know that's best for us both, but I can't bear to have you ashamed you wanted my love to comfort your sorrow – when I'm so proud I could give it. (*Pleadingly.*) I hoped, for your sake, you wouldn't

remember, but now you do, I want you to remember my love
for you gave you peace for a while.

TYRONE (*stares at her, fighting with himself. He stammers defensively*).
I don't know what you're talking about. I don't remember –

JOSIE (*sadly*). All right, Jim. Neither do I then. Goodbye, and
God bless you. (*She turns as if to go up the steps into the house.*)

TYRONE (*stammers*). Wait, Josie! (*Coming to her.*) I'm a liar! I'm a
louse! Forgive me, Josie. I do remember! I'm glad I remember!
I'll never forget your love! (*He kisses her on the lips.*) Never!
(*Kissing her again.*) Never, do you hear! I'll always love you,
Josie. (*He kisses her again.*) Goodbye – and God bless you!

*He turns away and walks quickly down the road off left without
looking back. She stands, watching him go, for a moment, then she puts
her hands over her face, her head bent, and sobs. HOGAN comes out
of her room and stands on top of the steps. He looks after TYRONE
and his face is hard with bitter anger.*

JOSIE (*sensing his presence, stops crying and lifts her head – dully.*) I'll
get your breakfast in a minute, Father.

HOGAN. To hell with my breakfast! I'm not a pig that has no
other thought but eating! (*Then pleadingly.*) Listen, darlin'. All
you said about my lying and scheming, and what I hoped
would happen, is true. But it wasn't his money, Josie. I did see
it was the last chance – the only one left to bring the two of you
to stop your damned pretending, and face the truth that you
loved each other. I wanted you to find happiness – by hook or
crook, one way or another, what did I care how? I wanted to
save him, and I hoped he'd see that only your love could – It
was his talk of the beauty he saw in you that made me hope –
And I knew he'd never go to bed with you even if you'd let
him unless he married you. And if I gave a thought to his
money at all, that was the least of it, and why shouldn't I want
to have you live in ease and comfort for a change, like you
deserve, instead of in this shanty on a lousy farm, slaving for
me? (*He pauses – miserably.*) Can't you believe that's the truth,
Josie, and not feel so bitter against me?

JOSIE (*her eyes still following TYRONE – gently*). I know it's the
truth, Father. I'm not bitter now. Don't be afraid I'm going to
leave you. I only said it to punish you for a while.

HOGAN (*with humble gratitude*). Thank God for that, darlin'.

JOSIE (*forces a teasing smile and a little of her old manner*). A ginger-haired, crooked old goat like you to be playing Cupid!

HOGAN (*his face lights up joyfully. He is almost himself again — ruefully*). You had me punished, that's sure. I was thinking after you'd gone I'd drown myself in Harder's ice pond. There was this consolation in it, I knew that the bastard would never look at a piece of ice again without remembering me.

She doesn't hear this. Her thoughts are on the receding figure of TYRONE *again.* HOGAN *looks at her sad face worriedly — gently.*

Don't, darlin'. Don't be hurting yourself. (*Then as she still doesn't hear, he puts on his old, fuming irascible tone.*) Are you going to moon at the sunrise for ever, and me with the sides of my stomach knocking together?

JOSIE (*gently*). Don't worry about me, Father. It's over now. I'm not hurt. I'm only sad for him.

HOGAN. For him? (*He bursts out in a fit of smouldering rage.*) May the blackest curse from the pit of hell —

JOSIE (*with an anguished cry*). Don't, Father! I love him!

HOGAN (*subsides, but his face looks sorrowful and old — dully*). I didn't mean it. I know whatever happened he meant no harm to you. It was life I was cursing — (*With a trace of his natural manner.*) And, be God, that's a waste of breath, if it does deserve it. (*Then as she remains silent — miserably.*) Or maybe I was cursing myself for a damned old scheming fool, like I ought to.

JOSIE (*turns to him, forcing a teasing smile*). Look out. I might say Amen to that. (*Gently.*) Don't be sad, Father. I'm all right — and I'm well content here with you. (*Forcing her teasing manner again.*) Sure, living with you has spoilt me for any other man, anyway. There'd never be the same fun or excitement.

HOGAN (*plays up to this — in his fuming manner*). There'll be excitement if I don't get my breakfast soon, but it won't be fun, I'm warning you!

JOSIE (*forcing her usual reaction to his threats*). Och, don't be threatening me, you bad-tempered old tick. Let's go in the house and I'll get your damned breakfast.

HOGAN. Now you're talking.

He goes in the house through her room. She follows him as far as the door — then turns for a last look down the road.

JOSIE (*her face sad, tender and pitying – gently*). May you have your wish and die in your sleep soon, Jim, darling. May you rest for ever in forgiveness and peace. (*She turns slowly and goes into the house.*)

Curtain.